Gems

Knowing Christ in the Light of Modern Wisdom

CORA EVANS

Gems

*Knowing Christ in the Light
of Modern Wisdom*

SECOND PRINTING

The Mystical
Humanity
of Christ
Publishing

San Mateo
2017

Gems
Cora Evans
© 2017 The Mystical Humanity of Christ, Inc.

IMPRIMATUR
+ Most Reverend Richard J. Garcia, D.D.
Bishop of the Diocese of Monterey, California
March 22, 2017

Published by The Mystical Humanity of Christ, Inc.
CoraEvans.com
RefugeefromHeaven.CoraEvans.com
SelectedWritings.CoraEvans.com
Sparks.FatherFrank.com

Book Title—Cora Evans selected the title of the book at the direction of our Lord as recounted in the writing titled "Our Lord's One-Hour Vacation into the World."

Cover design by Claudine Mansour Design, Mission Viejo, California
Interior design by Russell Graphic Design, Pasadena, California

Library of Congress Cataloging-in-Publication Data
Evans, Cora

978-0-9910506-7-3 Quality Paperback
978-0-9910506-8-0 eBook

Printed in the United States of America

Gems: Knowing Christ in the Light of Modern Wisdom is based on the private revelations of Cora Evans.

Public Revelation—Sacred Scripture

The Catholic Church recognizes the clear distinction between public and private revelation. Public revelation, meaning the Old and New Testaments, ended with the death of the last apostle. It is complete; the age of public revelation is closed and there will be no new public revelation.

It is no longer public revelation [Sacred Scripture] that grows, but we grow in our comprehension of it.

Private Revelation—
A Possible Means to Growth and Understanding

The purpose of private revelation is to help a particular soul grow in faith and to develop a greater love of God.

For even though public revelation is already complete, it has not been made completely explicit; it remains for Christian faithful gradually to grasp its full significance over the course of centuries. Throughout the ages, there have been so-called private revelations, some of which have been recognized by the authority of the Church [Saint Bernadette of Lourdes, Saint Catherine of Siena, Saint Margaret Mary, Saint Faustina]. It is not the role of private revelation to improve or complete Christ's definitive Revelation, but to help live more fully by it in a certain period of history.[1]

---

1   *Catechism of the Catholic Church* (65,66): Second Edition, revised in accordance with the official Latin text promulgated by Pope John Paul II in 1997.

RECOGNITION

The Mystical Humanity of Christ, Inc.,
Gratefully acknowledges the Extraordinary Generosity
of the
Theresa and Edward O'Toole Foundation
Bert Degheri, Co-Trustee

PUBLISHER'S ACKNOWLEDGEMENTS

The mission entrusted to Cora Evans by our Lord continues, and we wish to express appreciation to Most Reverend Richard Garcia, D.D., Bishop of Monterey, California, for opening the canonical inquiry into her life and heroic virtues and thereby declaring her Servant of God. We appreciate the work of the tribunal, canon lawyers, theologians and the historical commission. We wish to thank Fr. Joe Grimaldi, J.C.L., Postulator, for his inspiration and insight. Special appreciation to the family members of Cora Evans: Dorothy Evans, daughter and Bob Spaulding, nephew. Also, Irene and Mark Montgomery, June Haver MacMurray (deceased), and the trustees of the June and Fred MacMurray Foundation, Peter Marlow Jr., Bill O'Connell, Gabrielle Lien, and her late husband, Warren. Special appreciation is expressed to the Jesuits of the California province; Rev. Michael Weiler, S.J., Provincial; Rev. Vito Perrone, COSJ; and Rev. Gary Thomas for their spiritual support and advice; Michael Huston, advisor, retreat leader and board member; and Pamela McDevitt, for her encouragement and guidance.

LED BY OUR LORD

This phrase formally summarizes our journey. It is the motto that expresses the publisher's awareness of God's intervention as the mission entrusted to Cora Evans, to promulgate the Mystical Humanity of Christ throughout the world, unfolds.

Contents

INTRODUCTION

Take your time. I know of no other book like this one, a collection of the thoughts and prayers of a woman entrusted by our Lord to promulgate the Mystical Humanity of Christ—the divine indwelling (see 1 Cor 3:16)—throughout the world. She was instructed to write, and her soul was guided by a renowned Jesuit priest. This is a book to be read and reread, to be on your nightstand, to pray with in Church, and to discuss with friends.

What if you could come even closer to Jesus? You are about to encounter Christ with fresh insights into the love He has for you personally.

Michael McDevitt
Custodian for the Writings of Servant of God Cora Evans

EDITOR'S NOTE

This gift He had given me, better to express His life and infinite love in our world . . . where human words seem ugly and unrefined and appear to a soul in love with God like clumsy brushes in the hands of an artist.

It is truly a world with expressions but without words.

Cora Evans
Gems

An editor's most essential role, arguably, is to act as intermediary between the author and his audience. Depending on the medium at hand, the editor clarifies, elucidates, corrects, and occasionally shapes the words on the page, acting to bridge the space between the creator's thought and the reader's understanding.

All very well for nonfiction and fiction manuscripts. What, then, is the role of an editor confronted by the words of a reputed mystic and visionary, whose express purpose in writing is to convey divinely revealed messages?

Cora Evans struggled with the limitations of language to recount what cannot be captured in words. For her, the writer, conveying in finite language the ineffable truths that lie beyond the comprehension of a fallen—and therefore darkened—mind was nothing if not daunting. Her response, plainly stated in her own words, was to seek earnestly to become ever smaller, indeed, to ache for nothingness, so that the beauty of the Eternal might shine through, even though His instrument be imperfect.

I am instructed by Mrs. Evans' own difficulties and by her response: humble submission to the task, mindful that her gifts were given to serve God's design, to be one more "link in the chain," as she eloquently characterizes it. Never has that maxim been so explicitly set before me as on this project. Indeed, even as I worked to render her meaning as clearly as possible, I found myself backing away from long-held practices, lest I run roughshod through spaces where angels might tread with caution.

The editors' mandate is to approach every text with objectivity, whatever our personal response to the words on the page. In this case, my beliefs about the authenticity of a private revelation are irrelevant to my task. And yet the more I read these passages, the more I seem to hear a still, small voice: *Get out of His way, and let the words—the Word—speak directly to hearts.* I hope I have succeeded, but I accept full responsibility where I have not. My trade is words; faced with the world "with expressions but without words," I must be the clumsy brush or else a barrier to the message.

Sophia Hart

PART ONE

Gems

1938

HIS QUEST FOR LOVE

At dawn, in the quietude of silent prayer, I heard the deep, melodious tones of an organ and the voice of our Jesus singing His song of love for us on earth, "I love thee truly, My children." From within the miracle of spiritual eyes, I beheld our Beloved's voice taking a symbolical form—resembling long, waving, white satin ribbons flowing from the center of a great sun in the Easter sky. As each ribbon rippled in the heavens' air toward me, a white dove rose from each rise and fall of the ribbon waves until a thousand doves circled in the skies' immensities, there to form a banner which read in letters formed by slow-moving doves: "Blessed are they who hear the pleadings of the eternal God in His quest of love." From each written word in the sky flowed a mist of sparkling jewels, in colors of red, green, and gold. They scattered over the earth resembling a profusion of flowers, and I understood, with God's gift of understanding, that they were the symbol of His graces for His friends. These had heeded His song and returned His love by daily visiting God in His Humanity in His prison home: His tabernacle, the altar home on earth.

TRUE MAN IN TRUE CHEERFULNESS

Beloved Jesus, I believe Thou art true Man as well as true God, true Man in cheerfulness, true Man in understanding, and true Man in kind good humor. Yet the world and history-keepers teach us You were never known to laugh. Jesus, I find this hard to believe, and now I trust I am not offending Thee.

Jesus answered, "Child of beautiful faith in My Humanity, listen to thy reason for it tells thee I did laugh. All good men laugh, even though at times their hearts do break with sadness. In My public walks along the streets, journeying in and out the temple, or on errands for My Mother, it is true My smile was seldom seen, for it was the custom of the day to keep quiet dignity in public places. In My Mother's home, as well as my friends' homes, My voice was heard in laughter. Always remember, I give grace for happiness and joyous laughter, but never for smutty laughter. Offer Me thy laughter and joys. I love them as I love the sighs of penitent souls. My reward to penitent souls is oftentimes the grace of gladness, joy, and holy laughter."

1940

LITTLE CHAPEL, WAY UPSTAIRS

Jesus, oh so hidden in the little chapel room, way upstairs, Thou are in darkness and all alone, forgotten, kept like a Bible on a shelf. Dust does cover Thy altar home, and flowers are seldom seen to brighten Thy lonely hours. The evening air is still, and the gloom of clouds up high prevents the starlight filtering through to Thee. No melody of whispered rosary prayer is heard, nor a child's hurried step in search of Thee. Thy days are long and silent, Jesus, and in meditation's way, it seems I feel Thy loneliness in my heart. Thy eyes seem anxious in their constant watching for Thy prison keeper, Thy priest. Mystically Thy hands grow white with pain as they clench the bars of the prison doors. Thy smile is sad, Thy look downcast. "No visitors today," You whispered into my heart, "for the keeper of the keys locks all the doors after each sacrifice of the Mass."

Oh Jesus, my soul pleaded, please permit my soul to penetrate this Thy prison's darkened walls each day. Let me tell Thee in Thy mystical Humanity about the great outdoors, Thy neighbors and their joys, the wood, flowers, and the mighty pines. Permit my eyes as they gaze into Thine to tell Thee of my love for Thee in the measure of Thy loneliness. Permit my sighs to match Thy loneliness, and may each breath beg the Eternal Father for the grace of friendliness and gratitude to be given to Thy prison keeper. And may he see the necessity of open doors for the passerby who loves to say in his hurried moment, "I love Thee, Jesus." With open doors the children will say, "Jesus, we love Thee," and with their prayers and childlike laughter and stumbling feet, Thy hours of loneliness will be joyous in the little chapel, way upstairs.

1941

MY TABERNACLE HOME

Beloved of my soul, tonight in the nearness of Thy holy visitation, please enlighten my mind to the deeper meaning of Thy Mystical Humanity. Teach me how better to propagate Thy divine wish, the Mystical Humanity in all hearts. Our Beloved answered, "Many souls know Me only in the Blessed Sacrament in My tabernacle home, and only as a Little White Host. They do not realize in the Little White Host that My perfect Humanity is there as perfect God-man. Like of old in My Humanity, I abide by the desires and invitations of My people, according to the culture and dignity of each nation. I must be invited as a friend and guest into their homes through asking and receiving Me through the Blessed Sacrament. My delights are to be always with the children of men. I like to dine with them, and to be their close companion all the day in their work and home. With them I'll enjoy the day either in sadness or joy, and I'll be their guest and abide by their wishes. I'll enjoy the theater, concert, and symphonies, and the children's romp before bedtime. I would like to hear, in My Humanity, the children's fond, 'Good night, Jesus,' and welcoming words for My welcome as a guest again. My parting wish before I retire to My tabernacle home is the praying of the rosary to My Mother. For when I tiptoe into My tabernacle home, My Mother is there, waiting as all good mothers do, and I'll give her thy rosary as a token of My thanksgiving for the love and welcome given Me by My creatures."

1943

HOLY BLESSING

Oh, my Master, my King and holy Guest, how can I thank Thee for Thy great kindness in visiting me in this my hour of vigil keeping for Thy love? My Beloved's eyes pierced my soul with an understanding love, and He raised His gracious hand above my head and traced in the air the sign of the triple cross. My soul cried aloud, "Oh blessing divine, oh blessing sublime, make me worthy of Thy least grace and holy desire." Jesus spoke, "Child of grace, when thou dost bless thy friends, use a crucifix to imprint the triple cross upon their heads. Silently invite Me to dwell in thy soul to bless thy friends through thy body. And whilst thou dost bless with the crucifix, silently pray, 'I bless thee with all the desires of the Eternal Father and bless the wishes of thy soul, in the name of the Father and of the Son and of the Holy Spirit. Amen.'"

THOU ART A CHALICE

Today, my Beloved, I have offended Thee by the sins of exaggeration and uncharitableness in revealing my neighbor's faults and sins. Please forgive me, Jesus, and please forget my many sins. Give me the grace to place the word "Silence" across my lips. And when my lips try to move again in sin and the vice of much talking, please permit lips to feel the word of silence, as if it were Thy holy finger silencing me with peace and calm. Permit me the grace daily to kiss the earth for my own reparation and remembrance of silence, for earth doth not speak, but in the silence of order doth praise God continually.

In meditation's vastness of perfect rest in Jesus, I found myself walking beside our Beloved, and in the spirit we entered into one of His wayside chapels. There, on the high altar, He showed me a magnificent chalice before the tabernacle door. "Cora," He said, "Thou art a chalice, My chalice of loving joy. Would you not make haste to catch My Blood if It should overflow from the lip of the chalice in the Holy Sacrifice of the Mass? What would you think and how would you feel if I should tell thee My Blood was soiled by sins? Would not your sorrow plead with

Me to overcome sin? To thee, My chalice of earth, I say 'Let not sin enter into My chalice.' Let not thy lips open to words of sin, even in the least degree for, like you, when thou dost receive Me, I, too, gather all that flows from thy lips. My joy is great, and all Heaven rejoices when thy blood in sacrifice of crucifying sin glows in radiance and likeness to My Blood in the golden chalice."

FAITH IN THE NAME OF JESUS

Mystically it seemed I was walking on a long, tall stairway and, while I climbed, it seemed I heard myself repeating over and over, "I love Thee, Jesus. I love Thee, Jesus." As I reached the top, there stood our Beloved Jesus as though waiting for me. From His heart there glowed in crystal fires the Little White Host. I fell at His feet, better to adore our King in His Trinity of love. Suddenly it seemed as though I were encased in the sweet essence of love in the Little White Host. While in that sublime moment of love with our Master, He placed upon my finger a beautiful pearl ring. The large pearl was surrounded with a tiny black crown of thorns, so tiny against the glistening pearl as to cause one to think it was drawn with pen and ink, and from each pointed thorn there hung a miniature, blue diamond, numbering about seven in all. As I watched the pearl in its many changing hues, I suddenly felt the overpowering longing to become completely dissolved in God, and my soul in its dying moods called aloud, "Take me, Jesus. Take me to Thy heart. Take me from this agony of love even into nothingness. I cannot return to earth. Have mercy on me, my merciful Jesus."

As these words of anguish ended, Jesus spoke to me these words of joy, "I give to thee this ring, the symbol of beautiful merit, merit for thy love and devotion to the purity of intention through faith in My Name, Jesus."

THE CHINESE OUR FATHER PRAYER

One morning in the early hours of July 1943, I felt myself suddenly taken up in the arms of Jesus. There in His way of holy grace, I seemed to know I was in China listening to the sentiments and meditation of a Chinese soul as he said the Our Father prayer.

I understood that if a Chinese soul was going to pray for himself, he would begin the prayer with the words, "My Father." If the prayer was for the intention of self and others, he would begin the prayer with "Our Father." There before me, I watched the Chinese soul kneeling as though in the deepest meditation, and in God's good way I was permitted to accompany the happy soul in the view of his meditation. I realized his good thought: for the moment he was going to address his Creator. He felt the solemn occasion, and suddenly he was like a tiny child; before him in the far distant clouds appeared a massive door. It was tall and covered with jewels. It was the door to God in the vision of the Chinese soul. He ran quickly toward the door with his arms outstretched as though he were running into the arms of his mother, and all the time he kept repeating over and over again, "Our Father, Our Father, Our Father Who art in Heaven." As he neared the door, solemn words of love and adoration escaped his lips: "Father, my Father, Thou art behind the door and I am near Thee. How can I thank Thee?" Then, as the words "Hallowed be Thy Name" escaped his lips, he fell in adoration, better to reverence that holy and powerful Name of God. Then slowly he repeated the Holy Name of Jesus, knowing while he repeated it over and over that the great door would open to flood the light of God upon his frail body and soul. Slowly the great door opened, and the Chinese soul ran forward to kneel in the rays of God's light flooding upon himself and the world. With joyous heart he seemed to sing aloud, "Thy Kingdom of light doth now come upon this my earthly body. It is my earth bathing in Thy Holy light, better for Thy holy will to be done in this earth as it is Thy will in Thy Heaven. There, basking in Heaven's light, the Chinese soul quickly wondered what he should pray for and suddenly remembered there was only one thing on earth worth praying for—the continuation of the Holy Mass. And with outstretched arms to his God, he prayed, "Continue to give us our daily bread, the Blessed Sacrament, for through the Living Christ we gain all earthly sustenance, and oh great God, forgive us our sins as we forgive tiny children, and lead us not into temptation through Thy many gifts in earthly joys, for through them we may forget Thee.

Rather, dear God, teach us to love mortifications and the joy of practicing denials for the love of Thee. Amen."

1944

SINS FORGOTTEN

I cannot pray tonight, dear Jesus, because I am so saddened in the thought of my offending Thee today. I was very impatient with Dorothy,[2] and I scolded her severely, forgetting You would have spoken kindly. I penalized her, forgetting You are compassionate. I was angered because she hurried through her daily work leaving traces of neglect. To my sorrow, Jesus, I forgot Your charity and I angered Dorothy, leaving traces of darkness upon her spotless soul, and so I have wounded a soul for Thee today. Forgive me, Jesus. Again I beg, forgive me before I take my rest and, in the morning, I'll hurry to Thy priest to confess my sins.

After confession and while kneeling to receive our Blessed Lord, I said to Him, "I wish You could forget my sins as well as forgiving them, but how could that be possible? Thou art God, knowing all present, past, and future, yet I find myself wishing You would forget even more than my desiring Thy forgiveness." Jesus answered as He knelt beside me, "Do you remember Dorothy's first scribbling?" I answered, "Yes, Jesus." And Jesus said, "But do you remember each line and stroke?" I answered, "No, my Beloved." And Jesus said, "That is the way I forget."

Trust in His Promises

During Mass one Monday morning, I felt a strong urge to enter into the confessional. I wondered why, because I had gone to confession the previous Saturday. Still, I heeded the inspiration, and upon leaving the confessional, I heard our Master's voice within the depths of my soul saying, "Come visit Me this afternoon near My tabernacle home." In the afternoon, as I entered through the church doors to keep the invitation of our Master, I noticed a priest walking back and forth across the sanctuary close to the Blessed Sacrament, reading his breviary for the day. As I walked toward the communion rail, thoughts

2   Cora's youngest daughter, 14 years old at the time

of rash judgment toward the priest came into my mind. I judged him as one filled with pride, vainness, and presumption for reading his office while walking so near the Blessed Sacrament, which caused me to have worldly distractions rather than peace in hidden prayer with our Beloved.

Suddenly I remembered I had accused myself of those three sins in the morning confession. I bowed my head in shame and asked God's forgiveness for my thoughts in rashly judging His priest when I was guilty of those same sins. The priest reading his office turned and walked toward me. He was our Jesus Himself. He smiled and said, "I surprised you. Be at peace. I asked you here to give you peace. You confessed three sins this morning. Please repeat them to Me again." I answered with great sorrow of soul, "Beloved, I have sinned, sinned so many times in pride, vainness, and presumption. Forgive me, Jesus, and teach me how to overcome those sins."

Our Jesus answered, "Cora, I am going to flood your soul with the grace of understanding, a grace which I usually give only to the dying. Remember I am giving you this light of knowledge for yourself and your friends." Our Beloved Jesus raised His hand in blessing over me, and instantly I seemed to be walking into all the paths of pride the world has ever known. Its avenues of joys and pleasures, its paths of sorrows and despair—all led downward into terrible darkness toward the door of Hell. I felt and heard the evil spirits teasing and coaxing me to become one with them. Their promises were appalling. Their gifts of gold and jewels were overwhelming to the power of imagination. One promise seemed to hold me as though in a vise: Did I want power and recognition? As I seemed to fall into its path of earthly joy, I seemed to be looking upon myself as a tiny child, unkempt and dressed like a beggar, dirty and covered with running sores, and I was leaning against the black, charred door of Hell. I heard the child crying in a wild hysterical voice, "What shall I do? What shall I do?" Quickly I looked into the solemn face of our Jesus as He stood near me by the communion rail, and I said, "What shall I do?" Jesus answered, "It's so simple. Why do you hesitate to call on Me to help you, for you can do nothing without Me? Your cry should always be, 'Jesus, help me.' Cora, if you were to die this instant knowing thy sin of pride in its full understanding, where would you go, Heaven or Hell?"

I answered, "I would go into Hell." Jesus said, "Very well."

Jesus spoke into my soul, "Vainness was the second sin." Again I heard the evil spirits shout their words around me, "She is a soul in sorrow, a soul in despair, treading the pathway all poor souls must share. Her cloak of light in earthly vainness is now one of darkness, and in darkness she is one with us." I heard my soul pleading again as the child, "O memory forsake me. Oh memory forsake me. Oh light of memory, fade away, for thou dost teach me I loved my own strong will. I loved praise. I loved the vanities of the world." In vision's inner sight, I watched a little child dressed in golden satins, diamond pins, and bracelets and wearing a golden crown sparkling with emeralds which formed the world "Vanity" over the crown. The child cried bitterly, "What shall I do? Oh what shall I do?"

Again I looked into the sad face of our Beloved Lord and He said, "Child, there is nothing you can do to fight the sin of vainness until you learn that I am with you, in you, and by you always. Take the vanities of the world when they cross your path in the form of riches, flattery, praise, and secret desires, and adorn Me, who dwells within you, with all earth's gifts. Openly offer them to Me lest despair through vainness overtake thee. Cora, if you were to die this instant knowing thy sin of vainness in its full understanding, where would you go, Heaven or Hell?"

I answered, "I would go to Hell." Jesus said, "Very well."

The third sin of presumption was shown to me as the highest pinnacle of pride. As I knelt in sorrow before our Jesus, He asked me to repeat these words with Him, "Presumption is to steal from God." As I followed His words, I looked again into His saddened face and, to my horror, His Holy face was scarred and freshly wounded, and His cloak was covered with mud. Angry fingers seized our Beloved's crown of jewels and threw the jewels one by one into the terrible darkness. My eyes to the inner world of vision closed to the terrible scene of our wounded Jesus and again I heard His solemn voice, "Cora, if you were to die this instant, where would you go, Heaven or Hell?" I answered as before, "I would go to Hell."

Jesus said, "Very well," and as He spoke He walked toward His tabernacle home.

In sheer desperation and fear, my soul threw itself at His feet and with arms outflung toward Jesus, I cried aloud in great determination,

"I'll not go into Hell, Jesus, because I trust in Thy promises, and one of Thy promises is to forgive a soul in sorrow. Oh, Jesus, I am so sorry."

Our Beloved turned toward me and within a spiritual embrace of His love, my soul heard Him say with a voice of great joy, "Very well, run along home now and remember I chastise those whom I love, even in the inner world of quiet prayer. *Trust in My promises* is the main topsail on all clay ships as they sail on the seas of time. *Trust in Me* stills the turbulent seas of time; peaceful seas bring calm to souls and to you, Cora, I say, calmness of mind shall be greatly rewarded."

SPIRITUAL COMMUNION

In the holy hour of quiet prayer, within the twilight of Thy beautiful light in meditation's path, I have at last found Thee, my Jesus. Tremulously my soul breathes its way of love to Thee, and now in the sweet immersion of Thy beckoning love, I kneel before Thee, my Jesus, as Thou dost hang in majesty upon Thy cross. My soul cries out to Thee. How can I thank Thee for suffering for me? How can I show my appreciation for Thy great gift of faith given me in the hour of my conversion to Thee and Thy holy institution? Oh teach me, Beloved, how to teach and prove for Thy creatures who know Thee not that Thou dost really live. Oh Jesus, help me.

As my soul ventured nearer and deeper into His way of love in the quiet hour of prayer, I was permitted for an instant to gaze into His magnificent eyes where beauty, vastness, and knowledge are the essence of one meaning—His Love. As His right arm seemed to lift itself from the cross to encircle my trembling body, Jesus spoke into my soul these words: "Make the chain longer." I seemed to dissolve into a veil-like, soothing liquid fire where appealing grace in God's joyousness breathes in unbroken affections upon all who enter there. Hidden in the Sacred Wound of love in His side, I received our Blessed Lord in the form of the Little White Host. It fluttered like a wounded dove against my heart as though It were pleading for mercy to be awakened within my soul, better to teach His countless souls on earth the meaning and understanding of His Sacred Humanity. As I began to leave the welcoming love of the Holy Wound, I heard Jesus speak again, "Make the human chain of My Humanity in souls longer and longer." I understood in spirit that our Blessed Lord desired us to receive Him often through the day and night in a Spiritual Communion. Through receiving Him in an act of love, we would become like another soul to join the long human chain of another Christ's Humanity dwelling amongst us.

MANSIONS OF JOY IN HEAVEN

Oh, darkness in finite venturing, thou are darkness, yet thy darkness is light as light. For thou are the sacred hood and stole of power in meditation through which all light transcends and mingles with interior knowledge, thus bringing doubts and fears to naught. Through closed eyes in earthly darkness, then into darkness wherein the eternal embrace of love clothes the soul in the cloak of detachment (knowledge, love, and charity), darkness is then made light by eternal light.

There in the darkness of motionless, awe-inspiring light, I heard my soul speaking as if it were another creation, away from the body which seemed to stand by in an ecstasy with all five senses meriting like a mirror the light of God into its deathlike sleep with God. My soul spoke these words, "Oh, eyes of my soul, thou art blind in the darkness of eternal light, blinded in unendurable knowledge which burns away all words of expression to that which thou dost see. Thou art blind, oh soul, to the quenchless splendors of God which attract and hold thee, oh finite soul, hold thee like a moth in flight to a glowing lamp in the darkness of night."

My body swayed in pathetic, absorbing love in God and spoke aloud as it glanced upon the light in my soul, "Oh light of Heaven in my soul, as thou dost reflect thy joy back to God, please find and hold finite mind expressions, better for me to borrow and use for God's honor and glory."

Bathed in God's light, my soul sped away like a wounded dove lost in His immensities toward the sheen of eternal splendors—wounded because words to describe such a holy sight were foreign to the soul's knowledge. Slowly, I bowed to the weight of my nothingness and sighed as though dead, yet with a feeling of gladness to be nothing;

yea, even glad the expression of knowledge had not touched into eternal silence. Lower and lower into nothingness with silence and knowledge without words as friend, I suddenly found myself as a wounded dove in the palm of our Master's hand.

Cradled in His hand, I felt the light touch of His love, caressing the ruffled wings made bare in their flight to Him. His calm voice spoke with all merciful kindness, "Child of grace, thou art wounded, wounded as all souls are wounded who find Me in God's quiet meadows where crystal springs of great grace give new life to all virtues.

"Thou are wounded in the usual inadequacy of creatures' desire to express their perfect content in their finite venturing into the darkness of terrible light, which holds the heavens above the heavens and joys above joys in the degrees of light and joy in My Father's mansions, where empty thrones await earth's citizens who seek Me. Listen carefully, child of grace, to My baptism of words which I now pour into thy soul never to be erased. In these great degrees of joy, finite mind is incapable of remembering or speaking. Even petition is forgotten. It is here alone that I speak into souls the knowledge of love for Me. My gift to thee, child of grace, for thy great venturing to find Me is the thought of Heaven. There is only one Heaven, but Heaven has uncountable degrees of joys in God and these joys surround, as it were, the very center of Heaven, and each joy is known to finite mind as mansions. 'In My Father's house there are many mansions.'

"Citizens of Heaven enjoy God in the degrees of joy in which they worshiped and enjoyed God on earth at the moment of their death to the world. Some souls are dissolved in God, thus becoming one with the eternal Godhead or center of Heaven and enjoying the union of likeness of God. God's saints dissolved in His eternal Godhead are those who accepted My invitation, 'Except you drink of My blood and eat of My flesh, you cannot enter into the Kingdom of Heaven.' The Kingdom thus spoken of is the center in finite understanding, the heart of God. The heart of God is a restricted Kingdom, restricted for those who have allowed Me to dissolve in them whilst they sojourned on earth, thus preparing them for the great and final dissolving into the eternal Godhead at the hour of death. (Death, here spoken of, is death to all that is not in accord to complete dissolving into God, even souls' purgation in Purgatory.) This complete and final dissolving is a second death. It is the final purification and preparation—either on earth or in Purgatory—the better to become members in the particular kingdom where none may enter save those who have allowed Me to be dissolved in them while they lived no earth.

"Other souls look upon God or gaze toward the eternal light of God, as thou art now doing in thy finite understanding. Souls in these mansions or degrees of joy, always looking upon God, are known as members of God or citizens who are in Heaven gazing with all rapture and lights upon or toward the Beatific Vision. The degrees of these mansions are uncountable, yet souls experience no further desire nor power for higher mansions of love, but remain forever content with joy in its perfection for them. Their joy is eternal gratitude in the memory of God. Saints glory and marvel and praise God for, through the saints' charity, they are eternal members of God, for well they remember nothing on earth is done nor could be done to merit Heaven without the saints' prayers of charity. It is written, 'You are your brother's keeper.'

"When earthly death stills the hearts of men, they choose then the degree of joy or mansions, forever. No merit either on earth or in Heaven can add to the glory for a soul. For it is written, "As the tree falls so shall it lie." Prayers for the dead either from Heaven or earth are stepping stones for souls in purgation who are on earth or suffering in Purgatory awaiting the hour of complete dissolving into the eternal Godhead or accepting the degrees of joy or mansions which surround God." As the Master bid me goodbye in His embrace of love in gratitude for His creature's love, I felt my soul and body reuniting, better to stand the loneliness and atmospheres of sin on earth. All I could say was, "I love You, Jesus. I love You, Jesus, through love, for love, and in love. Nothing matters but love."

HERESY

Rosary of Little Brown Birds

In mental prayer, my body seemed to say aloud to my soul as if it were another person, "Oh, soul, thou are lonesome today, sorrowful and sad, walking alone and waiting for the Master's nearness to come to thee in the lonely desert of thy soul. Oh, soul, take courage and reject the impulse to relive and ponder over the footsteps of time gone by. Time is restless, restless as thy heart is restless in its search for God. The narrow path to God passes through the silent desert of detachment where loneliness in solitary stillness is the knowledge of one's own nothingness. In that nothingness of self, God relives His life in souls. The way is narrow and most difficult as well as hazardous. It is a pattern of life to follow. It is His way to travel to perfection and must be traveled with the care and faith a traveler with would watch his maps, better to watch the course the Master has chartered for thee."

I fell to my knees, and in spirit I felt the burning sands of time beneath me. In the depth of suffering in the world of detachment, I called on my guardian and guide, Saint Aloysius, for guidance and protection. I asked him, "Why do I feel the burning sands of time as I kneel in prayer?"

With a tone of gentleness and love, he answered, "Time does not stand still. Fear alone causes you to feel the sting of earth. Try to rise above the sting of attachment. Then you will better follow the Master's desires for you. The burning in your soul is the effect of repeated disappointments in life haunting you, causing you to offer excuses by the hour, thus doing violence to time and merit. Disappointments burning like stubble in your soul are like pagan fires burning before foreign gods. Cease now to honor useless gods. Rise above them by the hour as lessons for humility. The sting of earth when buried in the cloak of humility is dead. It is noiseless unless you allow fear to awaken it. Come with me into the heights of thine own soul where darker musings fade away."

I followed Saint Aloysius as one hastening in flight to leave the burning desert. I tried to walk in his footsteps. In doing so a thought of joyous gladness swept through my soul. Surely this was a game with God's saints, their little way in humble patience to lead us to Jesus.

Saint Aloysius spoke, "It is the Master's desire for you to follow me into your mission in life. You have been told your fighting in this life is against principalities and powers—great powers of evil which haunt the earth with repeated heresies."

Before us arose a great valley surrounded by high mountains. No flicker of light sped its way to us from its fabulous depths, nothing but the slushing sound of something which reminded me of breaking surf or waves slapping upon one another in their rise and fall with earth's ocean tides. As the eyes of my soul accustomed themselves to such terrible darkness, there in the center of the great valley, pinnacled into the sky, rose the spires of the Mormon temple. The slushing sound in and throughout the valley was the rise and fall of a million black snakes as they slapped and fell over one another. Their angry crawling and hissing at one another told my soul of hatred and their jealous watching to protect the temple heresy from the outside world.

As I walked along the top ridge of the great valley, I knew the snakes had knowledge of my presence. Suddenly and in anger, the million snakes (a million devils in the form of snakes) set their eyes on me. They swarmed toward the ridge where I walked. They hissed their fiery breath at me with threats of bodily harm and soul destruction if I did not cease praying the rosary for their destruction. For the first time, I sensed the power and use of the holy rosary over heresy and, as I walked along the snake-hissing valley, I prayed the rosary as I had never prayed its mysteries before. I prayed for the deliverance of souls held in bondage of heresy, for I had once been its victim.

In the path ahead and walking toward me was a priest. He was dressed in cassock with a purple stole around his neck. In his left hand he carried a black rosary and in his right hand rested an open book of prayers. We stood together looking over the valley of death and prayed the rosary. With the ending of each mystery, the priest raised his hand in blessing and made the sign of the holy cross over the valley of snakes and spoke Latin phrases which seemed to cause all the hideous snakes to seek shelter beneath the darkness of one another.

As the rosary prayers continued, the snakes, like tidal waves, swept toward us. They tried to climb the steep embankment near our feet, but the power of the holy priest and his Sign of the Cross caused many snakes to fall back into the valley as though dead. The bodies of the dead snakes seemed to formed a stepping ledge for the next oncoming tide of snakes in their attempts to reach us. Tide after tide rose and fell before us. Finally a few snakes managed to reach the top of the ledge. One great snake threw his head and body toward my feet from over the ledge. He missed my foot by inches and as he slid into the depths of death, the priest spoke to me these words, "Ask our Holy Mother to send the merits of her tears for us upon this heresy."

I heard my soul praying, "Oh, Holy Mother, lend us thy tears and, through their merit, aid and help us in this our fight with heresy."

Instantly the heavens rumbled and great floods of driving rain poured into the great valley, washing the snakes from their moorings on the mountain ledge. The valley filled with water, and then we watched the waters recede, leaving the valley washed clean with the exception of a few weather-beaten snakes who still clung to the temple doors.

Then I heard Saint Aloysius speak, as he seemed to stand near us, and tell me to follow him. I followed him into a glorious path of golden light where stood our Jesus, smiling upon us in His embrace of love where fear doth not enter in.

Three years later, on January 29, 1947, I felt within my soul the same terrible fear and broodings of mistrust against myself, the same fear and anxiety that I had felt when I stood near the ledge of a million devils, visioned in the form of black snakes. In this spiritual night of the soul, I tried to find ways and means of handing the torch of my mission—fighting heresy—to some other soul. I felt utterly helpless to face such a mission as spreading the Mystical Humanity of Christ and the hope of overcoming, through God's grace, the Mormon heresy.

I talked to Father Frank Parrish about my fears and doubts and asked for his advice. He assured me God would help me and asked me to continue with new courage and hope in my life's mission for Jesus. He also assured me he felt sure this was God's work with and through me. When doubts assailed me again, I must try to remember Father Frank as God's ambassador and trust in his judgment for the care of my soul and mission. This I promised to remember.

That same evening, I was assailed with greater doubts and fears, as well as thoughts of pride in the graces God had given me. I tried to believe and remember the words of hope and trust Father Frank had given me. Desperately I tried to believe and trust he was God's ambassador in judgment and power; yet I doubted.

I knew there was only one hope. I must go to confession, there to expose the secret workings of evil upon my soul. Then, in greatest sorrow, like sinking despair clutching at my heart, I knew I had offended God by not obeying and trusting my director to the utmost command of obedience.

On January 31, I made my confession and left the confessional with renewed hope and courage and with a peace that I have seldom felt or understood.

Two hours after the confession, I felt my soul drawn away into a spiritual embrace of love, there to experience new delights and joys that the world doth not understand. My soul returned to the sensible understanding and knowledge that I had been with Jesus, and remembered in the essence of knowledge I had promised Jesus that I would try to overcome fear and, with His help, I would pray for the souls hidden in the darkness of the western heresy.

Instantly I was again on the brink of the dark valley of death. Blackness had turned to a dull grey, which made it possible for me to discern the grey outline of the Mormon temple in a desert of awful loneliness. There before me stood our Blessed Mother, near the ledge where the priest had instructed me to call on our Mother's tears to flood away the terrible heresy (demons in the form of black snakes). She was arrayed in a glistening white gown, and in her hand reposed a blue rosary. Her beautiful fingers gently touched each bead. As she prayed, it seemed as if a snowstorm of glistening white crystals floated around her in countless circles, thus enclosing her in a cloud of shimmering mists. The snowflake crystals showered the earth at her feet. She asked me to gather them.

I knelt at her feet, and into a small bucket which lay on the ground I gathered the little snowflake petals of holy grace. When the bucket was filled, she asked me to pour the contents into the dark valley. I walked to the edge of the valley and did as I was commanded. There I stood watching the snowflake particles scattering over the dark crevices on the steep slope of the valley. As I watched their little light fall into such great darkness, I grew afraid with the thought that it would be impossible to fill the great valley with graces if poured from such a small bucket.

I hurried to our Blessed Mother's side to inform her of my fear and to ask her to release me from such a mission. Before I could petition her, she spoke to me these words, "Refill the small bucket, and empty it again and again into the valley."

I obeyed her request and, as I poured the second bucket of graces into the semidarkness, I felt again the terrible despair and utter uselessness of such a mission. Once more I walked toward her to tell her of my fears, but she kindly informed me to gather the graces again. As I knelt before her to refill the small bucket, I felt our Jesus hurrying toward us. He quickly knelt beside me and said, "Here, let Me help you refill the bucket."

I walked with Jesus to the ledge, and He poured the contents of the bucket into the valley. I noticed His ease, composure, and willingness to try to fill the valley—even if it did seem a useless gesture. As we walked toward our Blessed Mother, Jesus said, "I don't understand why you are so frightened at the valley. On Good Friday, I'll traverse the complete depths for your people. Will your frightened heart still the desire of My heart?"

My soul instantly fled to Him, there to dissolve for a moment into the warmth of His hidden love. There I asked to travel the depths for Him alone on Good Friday. I felt His heart was stilled in the inner peace in my heart.

It seemed as if in reward for my little willingness to please our Master, He told me He would be with me for about five hours on the fifth of February with further instructions and preparations for Good Friday.

February 5, near the hour of six p.m., my doctor[3] and his wife, Mary (Jessie), called on me for a visit. During the visit, I offered to read the writings on our Blessed Mother's hidden sorrow. As I began to arrange the papers, there above me appeared thousands of angels, in human forms of young men all dressed in beautiful flowing gowns of pastel shades and hues. In perfect order they seated themselves in a semicircle of golden chairs that filled the heavens from the eastern skyline to the distant western darkness. In the essence of knowledge, I understood they were going to listen to me read the paper on our Mother's sorrow. I could hardly read the paper. I was stunned with the thought of such an audience, an audience of angels listening to mere human words of expression on Mary's sorrow. Their golden light, like the hot rays of the noonday sun, gave me the feeling of being sunburned. I wearied under the heavenly warmth, and I felt my heart racing as if racing with time and death.

As I finished the reading and the heavenly vision dimmed before me, I seemed to understand that I had in God's good grace given joy

3   John J. McDevitt, M.D.

to the angels. They seemed to marvel that God's gifts were so clearly caught up into my soul, there to write them for His glory for souls on earth. As I folded the paper as one closing a book, my soul was again caught up into the heart of Jesus, and there we walked in the dusk on the ledge of the great dark valley. Jesus was dressed in a flowing green cape, lightly touched with purple and embroidered with silver threads. His crosier was jeweled in green emeralds, rubies, and diamonds. Jesus handed me His crosier, but its weight was impossible for me to lift. There we stood gazing upon the symbol (crosier) of power that I knew I must carry for Jesus on Good Friday into the depths of the western heresy.

Jesus picked up the crosier and placed it lengthwise across my outstretched arms. In this manner I was to carry His crosier into the dreadful darkness of death on Good Friday. My eyes followed His eyes into the valley of darkness as He seemed to be mapping my future course into the threading gloom for souls. The distance seemed long and frightening to my soul. Then Jesus spoke, as my eyes fell upon the doors of the temple. "Cora, you will walk three times around the temple in honor of the Holy Trinity. Each time, with My crosier mark the sign of the cross upon the temple door. Hundreds of conversions will be made this coming year through your efforts and your obedience."

As if to try to erase the fearful thought of Good Friday, Jesus spoke with great kindness into my soul these words, "Your friends, Dr. Jack, Mary, and Edythe (my nurse), are anxious over you. Return to them and after a while, I'll take you to My heart again."

To this request I answered Jesus in great pain, for bodily senses were beginning to reawaken from their sleep of repose in God, "I don't want to return. Please don't let me return. Let me stay with You, my Jesus. Let me travel the valley of darkness this hour for You. Then perhaps I can stay with You always."

To this request of pain, Jesus answered kindly (trying to reawaken my earthly mind to the gifts on earth), "Cora, your rosary sleepeth."

As Jesus spoke into my soul those beautiful sentiments of love toward the rosary, I noticed He held in His hand my little brown rosary. Each bead appeared as a tiny sleeping bird huddled closely to the silver chain of love. Jesus touched a bead on the rosary and began to pray the Hail Mary prayer and, as He did so, the tiny brown bird awakened and fluttered its tiny wings and flew away into the Eternal Father's light above us. As each prayer ended, the tiny birds flew away until the chain was empty, with the exceptions of the larger beads which did not resemble tiny birds in symbol meaning. As I opened my hand for Jesus to give me my rosary beads, I noticed in His hand was nestled another chain of sleeping birds. As Jesus handed me my rosary, He lifted His crosier from my outstretched arms, and we walked together as if back into the path leading to earth. I began to pray the rosary to please Jesus, but deep within my soul I was longing for death in Him, and so the tiny little brown bird just fluttered into the air and quickly returned to sleep again on the silver chain. Praying with added interest, I touched the next little bird, and it flew into a greater distance, but alas it, too, returned to sleep on the rosary chain.

Jesus said, "Pray harder."

I touched the next little brown bird and prayed with more fervor, and it quickly left the chain of love to fly higher and higher into the far heavens, never to return, for its purpose was with the Eternal Father. I sensed a feeling of joy, joy the fruit of obedience.

My eyes opened on the smiling faces of Dr. Jack, his wife Mary, and Edythe, who so graciously understood my mission of sorrow and joys. Without the vision of Himself before me, Jesus spoke into my heart these words, "I'll send Father Frank to you. He will help you carry the crosier into the valley of darkness. He will know and give the hour."

I visited with my friends for several minutes. I told them the beautiful story of the little brown birds and the second visitation which would come soon.

Again I felt my soul taken away into His beautiful light, as Father Frank and Mack[4] entered the room. I saw them and spoke to them as if through a cloud of white smoke, and then my soul was completely lifted from this earth into His embrace of love.

Later, as earthly senses began to reawaken themselves to the essence of earthly knowledge, I saw myself carrying the crosier on my outstretched arms as in the previous vision; however, I felt pleased as well as startled in the knowledge that the crosier's weight seemed

4   Cora's husband

light. Joy flooded my soul in the thought that perhaps my cross would be lighter on Good Friday—lighter and with less fear, better to follow the course of steps the Master had chartered for me.

Suddenly the crosier was heavier again, heavier than at any moment before. I felt myself bending beneath its weight, and in fear I looked up to find our Jesus and to beg His merciful help. There before me stood Father Frank dressed in our Lord's cape of white and holding the crosier. I was astonished to find it was as light as a feather, as long as I kept my soul's eyes on the cape of authority which Father Frank wore. I felt Father's blessings many times, and my soul was flooded with terrible remorse for ever having the slightest doubt in Father's judgment regarding my soul. Indeed, he is God's ambassador of trust and faith.

Immediately to the left of Father Frank, still dressed in our Lord's cape of trust, stood our wonderful Jesus. Again I pleaded to be released to go with Him. Again I reminded Jesus I would be willing to travel the darkness in the valley if He would only take me to Him this day.

His look was one of sadness, and again I felt the coursing, inconsolable grief within my soul. "I cannot leave You, Jesus. I cannot leave You," was all I could say.

Jesus sat down beside me and said, "If I take you with Me now, you will have less glory with Me forever." To this answer I seemed to shout as one in uncontrollable grief, "I do not want Heaven or any part of it. I only want to be a speck of dust clinging to Your sandal."

Our Jesus with tear-filled eyes whispered to me, "I do not like to leave you like this. Will you only trust Me? I know what is best for you," and then, as if to interest me in something of earth, He gently reawakened my earthly mind to the thought of my friends by saying, "You love Jessie, too, don't you? Dr. Jack would be surprised to see his own halo. Ask him to leave you a stimulant. You will reach a very low ebb tonight. I trust Edythe with all your gifts. Now I bless all your personal friends. Will you now return to give them My love and devotion?" I nodded that I would. Jesus then handed me the crosier. It was very light, and for a second I experienced great joy and love, joy to better please Jesus above everything else.

Jesus then asked me to step down two steps into the valley of darkness. There I would stand in spirit with His crosier until Good Friday or until Father Frank gave me further instructions. As my eyes opened to the earth again, I heard Jesus repeating over and over again one word: "Write, write, write."

1945

JESUIT DIAMOND AND
THE HOLY SPIRIT

I humbly kneel before Thee, oh mysterious eternal bliss, and everlasting gift for souls, as a wretched sinner, covered with doubts, despair, and mistrust in my spiritual director. Forgive the sins of my tongue, for I know I have been uncharitable in word and thought against a priest.[5] Please, oh Holy Spirit, accept the merit from the crosses and trials he has given me the last two years as a returning gift for his soul. May they help along the way to instill sanctification and peace within his soul.

If it is Thy will, oh Holy Spirit, for me to be guided directly by a priest in Thy Church, please lead me into the path of Thy choice. If Thou dost lead me to another director, please lead me to know who is graced with kindness, for well I know the depth of my own littleness. If is it Thy wish for me to return to the one I have abandoned, then it is Thy will, not mine and, in humble subjection, I'll kneel before him and ask his pardon for ever desiring lighter crosses from his hands. Oh Holy Spirit in the eternal bliss of the Eternal Father, come and help me, for I know I have received graces which I am unable to carry alone without the help of a director and the power which he holds.

As I raised my eyes to a heavenly picture of our Lord's beautiful Face, there before me I looked into a great distance and from that terrible distance winged toward me a white dove. In His mouth reposed a huge diamond, and I instantly understood it was a gem from our

---

5   Publisher's note: Although Cora does not mention him by name, she is referring to her former spiritual director, Father John Higgins. In a letter, Cora asked a friend to "Pray for Father Higgins. He needs prayers badly; he isn't so very well, and when you think of Father Parrish, just praise God and thank Him that He has given such a wonderful priest to the world." In 1963 Father Higgins abandoned the Catholic Church and was ordained a bishop by Michael Collin, a man falsely claiming to be Pope Clement XV. Collin had been a Catholic priest and was excommunicated by Pius XII in 1951.

Lord's Jesuit necklace. The brilliance from the diamond blinded me until I could not see the dove, but round the diamond as though written in golden ink, I read the inscription, "Father Frank Parrish."

All I could say in gratitude was, "Oh make me a mere reflection in Thy sight, oh Holy Spirit, just a tiny reflection of Father Frank's goodness, charity, and love. Give me the grace to be his willing follower as I follow his way to Thee."

JESUIT NECKLACE

Oh my Beloved Jesus, bless Thy holy priests, the Jesuits. Keep them free from sin. Especially bless Father Frank Parrish. Bless him with Thy grace of love, better for him to be Thy faithful imitator. Bless his every footstep and each heartbeat with Thy song of love, "I love thee truly." Hourly embrace him in Thy shroud of perfect peace and imprint upon his soul thy glowing grace of love flowing from Thy Holy Wounds. Sanctify his every word, look, and gesture, for he is Thy Image, Thy earthly priest, and keeper of Thy prison home.

Jesus answered me with a smile as He unfastened the clasp to His cape, better to show me a huge diamond necklace hanging round His neck. The glowing brilliance dimmed my eyes as I knelt in adoration and joy because Jesus seemed to find great pleasure in venerating each diamond with the fondness of a mother's love. Slowly and with great reverence Jesus said, "These are My Jesuits."

SKIES' CATHEDRAL AND
FATHER PARRISH

Oh hour of solemn quietude in the Holy Mass, how can I welcome thee? Oh hour of the holy Voice of inspiration, take me away in Thy shroud of prayer into the city of vision in the joys of the skies' cathedral. Oh skies' cathedral, thou are our Blessed Mother's home and refuge of sinners, as well as those who love thee, Holy Mother and thy Son. Oh Blessed Mother, penetrate my soul with the longing to be in perfect union and love with thee forever and ever. Oh hour of sublime love, adoration, peace, and worship, permit me to find through thee today a costly gem, a gift for Father Parrish, to show my appreciation and gratitude to him for his kindness to my wavering soul. For Father, I would choose a gift of beautiful light, a light that darkness cannot touch, a power of light better to shield him from the world's contagion as he tries in merciful charity to lift the many heavy crosses from weary souls. Permit, dear God, the gem to sparkle with grace of perfect quiet prayer wherein Father's words, deeds, and actions may lead him into a deeper dissolving love within the Sacred Host, our Hidden God.

Down and through the great cathedral's silent corridors and silent winding paths, I prayed for the holy gift of deeper prayer for thee alone, Father Parrish. From a great balcony, I looked into the space of immensities where stood broad canyons, rolling meadows, tiny lakes, and rippling crystal streams, and there on a sloping hill, standing in the circle of a glowing crystal rosary, stood our Blessed Mother with her holy Infant Son cradled in her arms. As I spoke my petition for you, Father Parrish, our Blessed Mother smiled and from her eyes fell two tears. They splashed upon the crucifix on the rosary encircling her feet. I quickly knelt in reverence to kiss the holy tears and, as I knelt, I heard a sigh and prayer escaping from their crystal depths, "Atone, atone for the sins of youth." Her holy tears were shattered in a hundred fragments, covering the holy cross like a mist of dew reverberating in a trembling way into incense which continually rose toward the cathedral's spires. Silently and in reverence, I gathered each fragment of the broken tears and kissed them one by one, placing them into a golden chalice which our Blessed Mother held close to her heart instead of her Infant Son. The ruby glow of our Savior's Sacred Blood within the chalice cast its shadows toward an altar where you, Father Parrish, offered sacrifice for love and penance for the world and its youth. As you lifted your eyes toward Heaven, your crown's inscription read, "Youth's pardon in sacrifice," and again I heard the deep melodious sigh from our Blessed Mother's soul, "Atone, atone for youth." She whispered into your soul, Father, as she handed you the chalice containing her precious tears mixed with Her Son's divine Blood.

JESUIT RUBY CHALICE

Jesus dear, I—Thy most lowly creature—wish to thank Thee for Thy great gift given me in body and soul this morning in the beautiful sacrifice of the Mass. I know and believe and find delight in the faith that Thou dost speak Thyself through the voice of our priests in a divine possession: "This is My Body and this is My Blood." When Thy beloved son, Father Parrish, lifted the chalice this morning for us to adore Thy Sacred Blood, I saw Thy glorious right hand in the place of Father's in the glow of Thy divine possession. Thy fingers were covered with Thy ruby rings, and from the flow from Thy Hand in Heaven's light, I was filled with the grace of peace, joy, and love for all Thy creatures. I wish to say, Beloved, I thank Thee.

Jesus spoke within my soul these words, "I love to give thee unexpected delights because thou dost never fail to tell Me all the details of thy happiness, as if I did not know thy heart's delights. My Humanity loves thee and, in a human way today, I wore for thee My ruby rings to match My chalice which Father Frank held aloft for thee."

JESUS, OUR GUEST IN LITTLE THINGS

Today at Thy holy banquet I asked Thee, my Jesus, to be my guest for the day in a very special way in Thy Humanity and perfect nearness. It is now in the afternoon, and I must ask Thy pardon and be excused for an hour, for a most severe headache seems to prevent my visiting and loving Thee as I would like to throughout the day. Please permit me to offer Thee my pain in union with Thy sufferings when Thou didst suffer from the crown of thorns for me.

As I rested, the pain seemed to become more intense and I said aloud as one would say in prayer, "I wish Mack were here. Sometimes he rubs my head when I am in pain." Our Blessed Lord spoke and I saw Him looking at me with eyes of sadness and pity because I suffered pain. "Little child," He said with great kindness, "Mack is not here, but I am your Guest for the day. Permit me to stroke your forehead." I felt His smooth, calm, gracious hand stroking my forehead in three long, smooth strokes, and I was instantly taken into His calm of perfect rest and sleep. Oh, I thank Thee, Jesus.

ODOR OF ROSES IN THE CONFESSIONAL

I humbly kneel before Thee, oh Little White Host in Thy tabernacle home, and humbly beg of Thee to come into my soul and earthly body as the Holy Infant Jesus. And while I hold Thee, oh tiny Infant, in my arms in the gift of meditation's prayer, please permit my tears to fall upon Thy tiny hands to tell Thee of my sorrow for offending Thee. I am so weak, so little, and so terribly sinful that I can only face Thee in Thy Holy Infancy. Forgive me, little sleeping Jesus. Would that I could never hurt Thee with sin, for never has it been known that one infant could hurt or harm another infant's soul with sin. Never leave me, Holy Infant. Stay in the cradle of my arms to ever remind me of Thy Infant frailty. Let all my tears as they touch Thy Hands form into a necklace of love, and on each bead let me write the words, "Forgive and forget." Oh, little Jesus, open Thy eyes to me, for without Thy gaze of mercy I am lost.

Jesus answered me as He stood near me in the magnificence of His grown-up Humanity. "Little child of My Soul, try to see Me in Father Frank more and more. Go now to him in My grown up Humanity and confess thy sins." I knelt and kissed the floor where He had stood and then entered into the hall of justice, the confessional. I heard myself as though I were speaking from a great distance, "Forgive and bless me, Father, for I have sinned." My eyes fell upon the profile of Father Frank's bowed head through the confessional window, and, as my sins rolled from my tongue, Father Frank was no more; Jesus Himself was sitting there in the confessional chair. Father Frank's confessional booth filled with the odors of fresh roses until one could see the cloud-like vapors rolling through the window into my compartment. I was speechless and could confess no more, but I felt my soul confessing in an act of love as our Jesus raised His magnificent hand in blessing over us. Gradually I could see the light of our Master's hand dim into the flesh of Father Frank's hand and, as His wonderful light dimmed away, He blessed us both with these words, "I love you," and I heard

Father Frank's voice speaking as if in answer to the wonderful blessing, "I am not worthy. I am not worthy."

FRANKIE BOY

Monday, November 19, 1945, I visited the Blessed Sacrament Church in Hollywood, and while there I prayed two rosaries before our Lord in the Blessed Sacrament. The first rosary was offered in thanksgiving to Jesus for His kindness in sharing with me His most precious friends, Dr. Jack, Mary, Anna, and Father Frank.[6] The second rosary was offered as an act of love to Jesus, petitioning Him to make me worthy of His great gifts (His friends).

As the rosary prayers and meditations on the mysteries ended, I felt my soul in the sudden immersion of our God's Holy Love. There, in His hidden protective love, I quickly looked for a crucifix in the church, as though I must hurry and kneel before it or die suddenly in the immersion of His great love.

At the right side of the main altar, near the communion rail, stood a huge crucifix elevated on the top of three steps. In spirit I quickly knelt in front of the communion rail before the crucifix and embraced our Savior's feet. As I kissed the sacred wounds, I noticed the right foot was alive, and dark crimson blood flowed from the gaping wound in the sacred foot.

As I watched the trickling blood, the church filled with the odors of roses, and thin music like darting wings of a thousand doves floated here and there around my heart. Then, like a thin haze among the odors of roses, rose the chimes of silver bells and, as they rang, I looked toward the Blessed Sacrament. There, as if coming from a golden light, walked a small boy toward the communion rail. His eyes were blue and his hair was a mass of short, golden curls, and from beneath the hem of his long dress, pink toes were visible as he slowly walked to the timing of the silver chimes. His flowing gown was white and soft as if made

---

6   The friends are John J. "Jack" McDevitt, M.D., his wife Mary, her sister Anna O'Neill, and Mary's brother Father Frank Parrish, S.J. (Cora's confessor and spiritual director). Mary and John McDevitt are parents of Frankie McDevitt (1938–1943).

from the sheen of lilies; it was girded with a golden cord. In his arms and close to his heart, he carried a huge bouquet of silver roses. Each petal seemed to be made of fine spun glass or silver, and each petal glistened with tiny diamonds which cast their prismed rays in all directions around the little boy, bathing him in a halo of gold and blue light.

Nearing the communion rail, he turned left and walked toward the crucifix where I was kneeling. Gently he placed his bouquet of roses on the floor and climbed the three steps better to embrace the sacred feet of Jesus. As his left arm encircled the cross and the sacred feet, he caressed the sacred wound with his small right hand as if to try to wipe the blood away. As he was thus caressing the sacred wound, he quickly glanced at me and asked, "Do you know who I am?" and then with a smile he continued, "I'm Frankie boy."

I was about to offer Frankie boy my handkerchief because I was afraid he would soil his hands and dress, when he smiled and said, "Daddy would know what to do with the wound, wouldn't he?" Then I knew he was Frankie McDevitt, and I quietly answered in amazement, "Yes, he would."

I leaned toward Frankie boy with my handkerchief and said, "You will soil your hand and dress; here is my handkerchief." With a smile on his face, he extended his tiny arms in imitation of Christ's arms on the cross, and his blue eyes seemed transfixed on the wounded right hand of Jesus. On Frankie's cheeks there glistened two tears. (I was given to understand one was for his Mother and one for his Daddy.) Frankie looked on his own little hand as if to show me there was no blood from the sacred wound to soil his hand or dress. And Frankie said, "I am one with Jesus and Jesus is one with me." With a beautiful smile he continued, "When you see my Daddy, ask him to bring all his temptations here, and together we'll hide them in this sacred wound, and I'll close the wound as I wipe the blood away, for Jesus and I are one. And remind Daddy when he feels the long thin pain piercing his own foot, he is in union and in pain with God and to say "Thank You, Jesus."

Frankie had completely wiped away the precious blood from the sacred foot, and again he showed me his clean white hands, and smiling joyfully, arose from the crucifix. He gathered into his arms the precious roses which he had placed on the floor a few minutes before he caressed the feet of Jesus.

I thought he was going to arrange them at the foot of the cross. I offered to help, and he answered with a most tender smile, and with a whispered tone he said, "These are my mother's tears of love for me. I have caught them up in my heart one by one and have guarded them all this time for her as my returning gift to her."

As he turned toward the main altar with his bouquet of exquisite tears, I said, "I'll give her the message, Frankie boy." As I spoke, I knew I would not have to give the message for the flowers were no longer in Frankie's arms. I followed the gaze of Frankie's eyes, and there before the huge crucifix knelt Frankie's mother arranging her own flowers around the feet of Jesus. Her look was sublime bliss and happiness in the gifts of a true martyr's love. On her head she wore a crown of sparkling rubies with formed the words, "Loving submission."

Frankie was now before the altar home slowly fading into his heavenly abode of light and, as he turned as if to say goodbye to the world, he said, "When my Uncle Frank raises the Holy Chalice, in Jesus I say "Hello and bless you, Uncle Frank."

My soul returning its earthly sense repeated aloud as if with a broken heart of unworthiness, "Oh make me worthy of the Thy friends. Lead me as Thou has led them to the sanctuary of love, the Blessed Sacrament."

CHRISTMAS EVE

Dearly Beloved Jesus, the lonely vigil of Advent is about to end. How I have missed Thee, my Jesus, and Thy nearness in the long, silent day of Advent in my waiting for Thee. I have missed Thy unexpected delights, Thy gifts to me in the knowledge of Thy Sacred Humanity, and now my soul is weeping tonight in loneliness for Thee. Oh, my Jesus, please come to me. I am hungry for Thee and my heart doth break for Thee. It is now in the early hours of holy Christmas morning, and I am remembering Thy promise given me before Advent that you would visit my soul on this holy day.

For a moment my soul seemed to be hidden in quiet prayer in the grace of giving adoration to Christ our King in spirit, when I felt the nearness of my heavenly guide and companion, Saint Aloysius. He gave me a blessing using the sign of the holy cross above my head, then handed me several huge, silver roses, fragile and exquisite in their tissue thinness, resembling the symbolic purity and beauty of mother-of-pearl. In the center of each rose reposed a tiny vial of clear, sparkling water. I was given to understand it was God's way of giving me permission to bless my friends with the grace of spiritual joy, through the power of one Hail Mary mingled with the gift of one drop of water to be mystically poured upon my friends.

Saint Aloysius led me, while I reposed in meditation's sleep, into the Jesuit chapel, leaving me alone before the main altar to kneel in adoration before the Blessed Sacrament as one in preparation to receive Holy Communion. I looked toward the tabernacle, and there stood Father Frank, his back toward me, dressed in cassock, surplice, and stole. For a second I had a fleeting thought of disappointment because I had expected at that moment to see our Blessed Jesus, and I spoke these words within my soul, "I thought I was going to see Thee, Beloved," and my Beloved answered into the depths of my soul these words, "I told you to see Me in Father Frank more and more." Father Frank then turned toward me, and my soul seemed to fade away into a state of remorse, shame, and sorrow for before my eyes, in Father Frank's body (our Lord's tabernacle), reposed the Sacred Host, our God and our King. Our Beloved's light of white and gold flooded the complete chapel and pierced my soul through and through. I felt an inner awakening of a newborn joy, peace, and consolation of happiness in union with God, and a better understanding of God dwelling within His priests (His other Christs on earth). The center of the sacred glow of light within Father Frank's body resembled a huge Sacred Host, the Blessed Sacrament. It was shielded by the black Jesuit crucifix over Father's heart. As I adored the Sacred Host within His human tabernacle, Father walked toward me as though to give me Holy Communion, but no ciborium rested in his hands, for they were folded in a gesture of prayer and quiet adoration. As Father stood before me, his right hand dipped into the depths of the magnificent white light within his own body and brought forth a tiny white Host, as from a ciborium, and gave me our Blessed Lord in Holy Communion. Father immediately returned to the altar and, after a few minutes in prayer, he turned again toward me, this time carrying a small monstrance wherein reposed a tiny white Host,

40

our earthly King and Eternal Father hidden in the accidents of bread. To myself I appeared as a small child and, as Father walked by me, I grasped his hand and we walked together into the space of time and darkness with the Little White Host as our guiding light.

Suddenly we were before the holy crib, where our Blessed Infant Jesus lay sleeping all alone, wrapped in His swaddling clothes and cradled upon exquisite shawls which shone with a brilliance of light in gold and black, like tapestries of great worth. The holy light from our Infant Jesus' body pierced through the wonderful swaddling clothes in a radiance of golden mists. In His light, I knelt more closely to the holy crib to better enjoy the flawless sewing and the royal purple embroidery along the edge of the exquisite hems on the swaddling linens. The linens seemed to be about two and one half inches in width and perhaps several yards in length. These bandage-like linens were snugly wrapped around our Savior's body and then over each shoulder time and time again, forming rhythmic bands of royal purple that reminded me of our priests' sacred vestments. His little, sacred head was also wrapped in narrower winding linens, forming three tall points in their exquisite folding and resembling a bishop's miter outlined in royal purple stitching, which I was given to understand was lovingly embroidered by our Blessed Mother for Her Infant Son. Our Savior's little arms were closely wrapped to His body under the windings of swaddling clothes, leaving just His tiny hands exposed. His tiny fingers seemed to move in a gesture of benediction, which made my soul weep over my sins of ingratitude in not respecting and cherishing His gifts both great and small. The cave and crib began to darken. The wall of rugged rock, the roof of straw supported by wooden poles, and the damp earth floor faded slowly from my sight, leaving the white glow of our Savior's holy light in the Little White Host in the little monstrance, once again our only light.

1946

MY LITTLE TRAILBLAZER

"Oh, my charitable Jesus of divine consolations, why am I so privileged in my utter nothingness to see and have the happiness of Thy sacred nearness in my soul?" As I asked this question, there before me spread a huge lake of ice, and Jesus Himself was skating over its smooth surface toward a golden beam of light that spread over the lake with countless other rays, as if they were reflections from an earthly sun. Suddenly I was a tiny infant resting in the arms of Jesus as He glided over the smooth ice fields. For a moment I had a thought of worry for the safety of our Lord if He should venture too near thin ice. As those thoughts rose in my mind, our Jesus stopped skating and showed me how He could chip the ice with the point of His skate. He said to me, "The ice is very thick. I can chip it and it will not break through. Cora, we are skating upon the ice of thine own soul. It is the symbol of your detachment from the world and creatures." As we skated on toward the great beam of light before us, I felt a sudden jarring in the smoothness of the ice. Jesus spoke, "That uneven space of ice was one of your rebellions against detachment, but it is frozen over now." We skated on and on and gradually found our way into the great golden beams of light. After we had skated some distance into the golden beam, Jesus turned His back to the great light and with delight showed me His skate marks on the ice. My eyes followed His, following mark after mark, and there, far away, emerging from the earthly, fog-like darkness of earth were hundreds of my friends following His skate marks into the golden path of eternal light. Jesus turned again toward the great golden light and, as we skated on and on, He said, "My little trailblazer."

JESUS WRITES IN GREEK AND LATIN

One early morning during vigil hour to adore our Blessed Lord, I felt within my soul His blessed nearness and, for a moment while in adoration to Jesus, I felt no longer a divided heart in the path of distractions between God and earth, but alone with Jesus. Alone I dwelt with Jesus in His possession of immeasurable love where transcend His affections and consolations to souls who try to love Him.

There, within His holy grace of exquisite delights, I was permitted in spirit to watch Jesus writing with a pen upon two sheets of paper. The language written on each paper differed in their characters, but I seemed to realize the message had the same meaning. I guessed—as one would guess in an earthly sense—that one language was Latin and the other Greek.

Jesus said to me as I knelt at His knee, "Receive permission to read them."

The following week I obtained the desired permission from my director, but from January 1946 until Good Friday 1946, I hesitated to ask Jesus for the hidden meaning written on the two slips of paper because of my unworthiness and wanting to prove to myself that I was seeking knowledge out of curiosity.

Early Good Friday morning during another blessed vigil hour, it seemed I was given the privilege to kneel in spirit near our Jesus in the Garden of Gethsemane. There in the stillness of night, the solitude of His quiet way in the illumination of seraphs' glory and light, where constantly transcend the Eternal Father's gifts in wisdom, understanding, and love, Jesus and I talked to each other.

Now my soul cries in defeat as I try to call into words the wondrous moment in Gethsemane. My soul seemed to plead to the nothingness of myself these words, "Oh hour of sublime beauty, oh hour of sublimest sentiments, how can worldly mind comprehend His magnificent voice and the gaze of His sorrowful eyes? Oh my soul, it seems thou hast failed me, for mere words cannot recapture one tone of His voice, nor is there one word to describe His tears. Oh hour of sublime magnificence, would that I could leave you as a sleeping child in death to remain forever undisturbed, but it is the will of holy obedience that I try to recapture for my friends the dust of knowledge hidden beneath the Master's feet.

There, in the captivity of His world where human speech is unknown, I understood it was our Beloved's desire to give me the knowledge and understanding of His letters written in Latin and Greek.

A moment later, within the embrace of His love, I understood Jesus to say, "Latin is My symbol for the universal language. Greek is the language known by few. It is the symbol of the spiritual life in Me. For the world to know Me as I desire to be known, the Greek language, or hidden spiritual life in Me, must be translated into everyday, universal language using words of simplicity, joy, and love."

"My desire is to be a constant companion in the souls of My friends and, unless they receive Me in the Eucharistic Bread, where I am in Person, I cannot be their constant companion except in memory or desire. I desire My creatures to know that I am real, and I am a lonesome God on earth because my Humanity is not known, nor believed, nor lived. Yet every generation has heard My song, 'My delights are to be with the children of men.'

"If My creatures would only take Me into their souls and ask Me to be their constant companion, much of earth's evils would cease. The taverns of vice would close for shame because My companions would refuse to take Me into places of sin. Instead of places of sin, My companions would choose for me wholesome entertainment.

"My creatures fail to understand: they are a living chalice, the chalice or real home of the Holy Spirit. And that living chalice was blessed and consecrated with the greatest care and devotion, even greater than the golden chalice used in the Holy Mass. But alas, those same children take their holy bodies into the dens of evil, there to become soiled, bruised, broken and even spit upon. I ask them, would they not hide in shame? Would they not make great acts of love in reparation, and would they not fight as for life if they, in those dreadful moments in places of sin, should chance upon a holy priest with chalice in hand walking into a tavern of evil and at the bar drinking unto himself a toast in the midst of cursing, drunkenness, and lust? Yet I say that golden chalice in the priest's hand is not real. It, too, will die with the world, but My chalices, the human body, will never die, for they are blessed and consecrated tabernacles, homes for the Holy Spirit.

"The Holy Spirit hidden in His human chalice is always accompanied by thousands of holy angels. Oh My humble servant, tell My creatures to be thoughtful and careful where they take the Holy Spirit, for often, in and through those places of sin and desecration to His holy home (the human body), the Holy Spirit pleads with the Eternal Father to open the doors of justice upon the earth. Justice would and could consume the world with vengeance but, through willing souls who have taken Me into their souls, through them I plead to the Eternal Father for mercy. And the light of My Resurrection in souls stays the hand of the Eternal Father, and justice turns its million eyes away from earth."

I heard my soul praying as I left our Savior's side in Gethsemane and, with fear and trembling, yet with firm resolve, I promised to teach the real living Jesus, the real Human God-Man amongst us. As Heaven's light and understanding wavered before me, leaving me alone on earth, I fell into deeper prayer and sighed this prayer to the divine memory of His sublime goodness, to teach us His hidden life, his wish to make His life understood by all, His desire to live within us His divine life. "Oh radiant heights of love, Thou are purity, and through the purity of intention and purity of real life, we live again for Jesus, live for His joy, live for His love, live to die with Jesus. Oh purity of soul, help me die to self when I again live in His possession of immeasurable love, where transcend His affections and consolations. Oh Jesus, take Thou all my will, my love, and my devotion to make Thee more alive in my humanity which I now give to Thee for Thee to purify and then to live within."

ROSEBUD WITHOUT LEAF OR STEM

While praying the rosary and offering each bead as an expression of love to our Blessed Lord, I suddenly realized my thoughts and desires had not followed the beautiful path of meditation on the sacred mysteries. My soul felt the pain of inward sorrow for such neglect, and quickly I resolved to amend my ways in the paths of meditation. I felt as though my soul was clothed in a cloak of sorrow, a cloak anyone would want to discard, for over its many folds were written the words, "Neglectful soul, neglectful soul."

I kissed the earth in reparation and pleaded with my Master to wound my heart with a dart of pain, ever to remind me of my sin of neglect and my promise to amend my ways of error. Instantly I felt my body and soul resting in God's holy gift of quiet prayer, where human words are meaningless and where only thoughts in sentiments of love are really heard. It was then I noticed our Jesus standing beside me as I raised myself from the gesture of kissing the earth.

His gentle, quiet way taught me that our Jesus was troubled. His concern at the moment seemed to be a very large rosebud resting in the palm of His magnificent hand. I watched Jesus turn the rosebud over and over as though studying its hidden meaning.

These thoughts arose within my soul as I watched Jesus turning the rosebud, "I find these rosebuds most difficult to arrange for My Mother. Perhaps you have a suggestion?"

As Jesus spoke, my gaze fell toward His feet and, to my surprise, there He stood in a profusion of rosebuds, all without stems and leaves. I was given to understand the rosebuds were symbols of my poor prayers in praying the rosary, incomplete because I had not curbed my mind in its wanderings over trivial, earthly affairs. There I knelt, gazing up on my poor prayers, roses of little use or worth because I had failed to complete the rosary prayers with thoughts of meditation. Again I begged forgiveness for my sins of neglect and asked Jesus to return the rosebuds, better for me to complete the prayers in earthly time. Jesus answered me in the depths of my soul, like a breath of love in forgiveness with these words, "You may complete the rosebuds with stems and leaves by and through the grace of joy you receive when you recall to mind the meditation on the Chinese Our Father prayer."

BILOCATION IN CHINA

In a lonely hour in a spiritual night of my soul, I prayed aloud these words, "Nothingness, oh nothingness of my soul, truly thou art nothing without the Master's gaze of love. Oh Jesus, in my helplessness please protect me with Thy grace of compassionate mercy and build 'round my soul a spiritual shroud where earth's distractions cannot enter in and where only good thoughts and prayers of love may rise to greet Thee, Beloved of my soul."

Then, as if in answer to my prayer and in His compassionate mercy, I was reminded to receive Jesus in the Little White Host in a spiritual remembrance in honor of His divinity. As I meditated upon the sacred majesty of the Little White Host alone in His altar home, I felt the nearness of our Beloved Master within my soul. Through eyes of faith in the grace of His mercy, I was permitted to see Jesus, our King, standing before me with the real Little White Host in His hand. Immediately I understood our Blessed Lord was going to give me the Blessed Sacrament. In the spirit of love, adoration, and praise, I received Jesus in the Little White Host and, while I lived in those blissful moments of love, I felt the Little White Host in my mouth retaining its crisp firmness, refusing to be moistened with my tongue. My soul fell into a state of fear—fear that I had received Jesus in mortal sin. In anguish of soul, I pleaded with Jesus to forgive me my sins as I knelt embracing His feet.

Jesus answered with a smile and the words "Fear not. I understand in your joy of ecstasy how reason is forgotten, and you would even mistrust My judgment. Do you love me?"

I answered with a smile, and then in a transport of joy within the embrace of our Beloved's love, I felt myself taken away to the land of China. I seemed to be kneeling beside a Chinese man struggling in the pain of a sudden death. He looked into my eyes and asked, "Who are you?"

I answered, "Just a friend of the Living Bread."

Gently our Lord raised the dying man's head from the ground, better to rest in His arms as Jesus knelt beside him. And while Jesus thus held the dying man, He caressed him as one comforting an ailing child. Little did the Chinese soul realize our Beloved's invisible, embracing nearness, and while Jesus held him close to His heart of love, the Chinese soul told me of his lifelong impatient longing and waiting for just one glimpse of the heavenly Bread, which he had heard about in his early youth from a missionary teacher. The sentiments of his Chinese words touched my soul with light and understanding as his eyes looked into mine, and I understood he spoke as one reminiscing through a past life of memories which told of joy, sadness, and desire in his constant vigil, longing for the heavenly Bread.

Our Lord closed His eyes, and His look was one of gratitude as we listened to the Chinese soul expressing his fondest hopes to me in these words: "In my youth I learned of a great miracle, a visible miracle on earth from God and how God knew we would be frightened of His great, incomprehensible majesty, and to arrest our fears, God found a way. He hides Himself in a little piece of Bread, better for His greatness to dissolve in us, better for us to become like Him. Oh, how I have longed and waited for just one glimpse of that miraculous Bread. How fortunate the nations are who have and possess the Living Bread of Heaven on earth. Tell me, woman, where do men find the Living Bread? Tell me about the castles men build for the Living Bread. Surely they must be the world's greatest and finest edifices. Does the Sacred Bread glow in a fire of white and gold? Does one feel Heaven's warmth when near the Holy Presence of God on earth? Does

God speak through the accidents of bread and, if so, what does God's voice sound like? Oh, woman, when men see the Flaming Bread of Heaven, what do they say?"

I answered, "Oh, most holy man of great desire, when one sees God in His accidental home on earth, there is nothing to say but 'I love you, Jesus.'"

The Chinese soul turned his head away from me as if searching for a moment of solitude where he could say aloud, "I love you, Jesus." As he turned his head, better to speak to Jesus, he looked into the eyes of his invisible Jesus, and like a child pleading in prayer, he spoke aloud these words, "Great God of all creatures, in my unworthiness if I have been presumptuous in my daily thinking and wishing for Thee to come within the gaze of my earthly eyes, forgive me for I know I am not worthy. If I have ventured too near Thee, oh Living Bread of Heaven, in either thought or desire, please forgive me. If my desire to see Thee, my God, hidden in a lowly piece of Bread is to remain just a desire, then I shall be content and die a man of desires, but I have believed and in vision's mind have pictured the glowing Living Bread as ever present and ever near me. Oh, God, forgive me my many sins as I forgive tiny children."

While the Chinese soul breathed his last breath, he called aloud, "Come, oh come, Living Bread of Life, I still believe Thou will come to me."

Jesus spoke to me these words, "Blessed are they who have seen Me in the Bread of Heaven, but more blessed are they who have not seen and have believed only through their eyes of faith. Give to my lowly servant the Bread of Life."

I took from my mouth the Little White Host, but it no longer resembled a Little White Host. It was glowing like a miniature sun in the sky. With trembling fingers, I placed the miniature sun into the mouth of the Chinese, and he breathed aloud through his soul, "Oh, great God of all creatures, Thy kingdom on earth, the glowing Bread has come into my soul. Oh, Living Bread, O living Jesus, bless China with Thy holy light of faith. I love you, Jesus."

Jesus lowered the humble servant's head to mother earth and, as Jesus knelt as though in silent prayer, from His eyes flowed two crystal tears. They fell across the stilled forehead in actual baptism by Jesus

Himself. Jesus spoke these words aloud, "Bless China through this man of sincere desire and blind belief in Me, for I am the Living Bread of Life eternal."

STATIONS OF THE CROSS FOR A FRIEND

For God's honor and glory and for our Lord's Humanity to be known among men, I willingly try, under obedience to my spiritual director, to recapture my thoughts, prayers, and gifts in heavenly manifestations to write them for God's glory through the Stations of the Cross.

With this simple prayer, I began the Stations of the Cross as I knelt before Jesus in his tabernacle home: "Oh Sacrament most holy, oh Sacrament divine, all praise and all thanksgiving be every moment Thine. Jesus, my Beloved, I wish to offer Thee my walk to Calvary with Thee to help gain peace and very special needs for my friends in Thee. My friends are Thy friends, and they have been very kind to me. Now, in gratitude for their kindness and charity to me, I come to Thee to ask for Thy holy smile of peace and love to fall upon their souls. One member of the family is Thine own holy priest. He is truly Thy living image in charity and kindness wherever he travels. The schoolroom, homes, or a sickbed, Thou are there, my Jesus, for he loves to take Thee wherever he goes, either in his person or at his side. His mother Thou hast called to the sublime state of holy widowhood to be more united in sorrows with Thy Blessed Mother. For this lovely widow and mother I plead with Thee to shower her remaining years with us with joys as only those in love with Thee can understand. I believe her daughters are rare gems from Thy eternal crown. Daily their souls reflect to other souls true simplicity, love, and cheerfulness. Thy crown, Beloved, must be dim whilst Thou dost wait upon their sojourn on earth. Bless them, Jesus, with such purity of heart that each day their souls will be Thy daily communion of joy in Heaven. And now, Beloved Jesus, this holy family has a son and brother who does not walk near Thee in Thy daily climb to Calvary. With this family in their sorrows over the son and brother, I wish to share the cross and burden. Permit me, Jesus, to assume he is my newly adopted brother, and now today I offer myself body and soul to accompany

Thee, Beloved, to Calvary in reparation for my little brother's neglect to Thee and to his family."

As I knelt in spirit at the first station, I felt the gentle nearness of our kind Jesus, and I understood He would accompany me in spirit to Calvary to help atone for His wayward son and my brother whom He loves.

Jesus spoke into the depths of meditation's sleep or drama within my soul these words, "My little son is on yonder hillside, tired and weary with the world. I'll carry him in My heart with us to Calvary. He is such a tired little boy, and on Christmas Day (any hour of his earthly death), we'll give him the spiritual gifts merited through our little walk to Calvary today."

At the second station I prayed, "Beloved, permit me to carry my brother for Thee. Let my heart be his silent Communion table. Bid my soul to take him daily to Thee in the Blessed Sacrament. Permit my soul to believe Thy holy smile has favored my sleeping brother." I heard my soul exclaiming aloud as I felt the nearness of my little brother near my heart, "Oh, baby brother, thy tiny hands are soiled. Let my tears wash them. And thy feet are bruised. Permit my lips to kiss and heal them. Thy eyelids are swollen as from crying bitterly. Oh, baby brother, why dost thou cry from loneliness when thou has God so near thee? Oh, my Jesus, I offer Thee my baby brother's hidden tears (his lined face tells me remorse has wept) as newborn acts of love. Oh, Jesus, forgive him and gently awaken him to Thee."

Gently, lest I awaken my little brother, I slowly walked toward the third station. There I watched our Jesus in the silent picture fall the first time. My heart slowly gave way to indignation toward all earth's executioners. For a moment I found no sorrow nor charity within me for sinners, and I wished even to abandon the sleeping child and run alone to Jesus. I fell to my knees and asked God's pardon for my own weakness and sin, for I was angry and uncharitable even in the presence of the Blessed Sacrament and toward a tiny child whom He loves and for whom He had just fallen beneath the terrible cross. All I could say as I rose to my feet was, "Bless this child in my heart, forgive me my sins, and please give me the grace of charity."

"Jesus," I prayed as we neared the fourth station, "Thou are about to meet Thy sorrowing mother. Jesus, when Thou dost turn to bless Thy mother, ask her to bathe this tiny child in one of her tears, for in her tears earthly sleep doth awaken as a new birth on earth. And, Jesus, please introduce this child's real mother to Thy most holy Mother, and may Thy benediction unite them as one in Thee. The holy little widow is near Thee, Jesus, in this Thy path to Calvary. She stands with arms outstretched toward Thee, patiently waiting for Thy favorable smile of grace to fall upon her ailing child. Now she bends to kiss Thy crimsoned footsteps in the sands of time with tears like diamonds telling souls the meaning of purity, hope, and resignation. Bless her, Jesus; she is my adopted mother in Thee."

With eyes raised to the fifth station, I exclaimed with joy, "I am so glad, Jesus, that someone is carrying Thy cross for Thee."

Jesus spoke, "Thou are helping my little son to carry his cross. I am as grateful to you as you are grateful my cross is lifted." In our Beloved's blessing of gratitude for my little help, I felt an inward peace and joy and hoped the little baby brother would always be my cross, for in his cross I had found joy in giving self and peace in knowing I was pleasing the Master.

Whilst I walked toward the sixth station, I prayed aloud in my newfound joy of hope, "Oh, Beloved Jesus, give my friends, the holy family for whom I pray, Thy blessing of love which imprints Thy holy face upon their souls, as Thy holy face was imprinted upon the towel Veronica offered Thee. I believe with the impression of Thy holy face upon their souls, they will fear no evil."

Jesus asked, "What would you give your friends?"

I answered, "Peace."

The Master continued, "My way would be a greater peace, peace of soul through resignation. Detachment is My way to real peace, detachment to son and brother in the flesh; consider the sleeping child for whom I was struggling beneath the cross. He is My problem. He is their cross through which to learn better resignation, detachment, and charity to believe I am a respecter of no person, loving each and every one, but hating sin in all."

At the seventh station, our Jesus had silently and painfully fallen again to His knees, fallen so deeply in the symbolic mud of women's sneers, while whispering, gossiping tongues splashed spittle upon the divine and holy face of Jesus. I prayed aloud, "Have I done this to Thee? Have I done this to Thee? Could I have prevented this terrible fall?"

Jesus answered, "Lift thou Me from this thistle-strewn path (gossip is the thistle wound to My bleeding flesh) into thine own heart of comfort, and there breathe thy prayer of charity for My little ones upon My scratched, bleeding flesh. Teach and quench unbridled tongues given to gossip to love and pray. Love will crush the thistle blossoms; prayer will remove its thorn."

In and through mediation's prayer, I found myself kneeling and praying with a group of women, all weeping because they loved Jesus and because He was suffering. They asked to have sufferings in their bodies, believing to suffer would lessen the Master's pain.

Jesus spoke kindly to all the holy women, and in His conversation we were made to understand His sufferings were for souls, not Himself, and to weep for Him was to weep for others, yes, even our enemies. Our Beloved's words rang through my soul with a new meaning, "Weep not for Me but weep and pray for your children, especially little children who have fallen asleep in Me. They are My cross of suffering."

As my footsteps neared the ninth station, I began to pray, but words would not come to my frozen lips, for my Jesus lay crushed beneath His cross, sighing heavily as one near death. Through His tear-filled eyes and sighing voice, I heard our Master speak to me these words, "Cora, gaze not upon this sorrow." I closed my eyes to the picture of His suffering and the Master's voice continued, "My eyes are blinded through the burning dust of the earth (pleasure). My throat is parched through intoxication (lusts of the flesh). My flesh is torn in shreds, and flies do eat and sting and build within Me their nests of filth. Oh, Cora, the symbol of neglecting vocation when I have called a soul to Me is the saddest of all sorrows. The flies and filth are truly the symbols of Hell. Pray always at this station for those souls chosen by Me for higher vocations. Souls living and loving their vocations are living and loving Me."

I knelt at the tenth station and wept bitterly because resignation in my own life and soul had not been cheerfully given. Given yes, but with reservations, which make me so ashamed, for He, our Beloved, asked for no reservations in and through His sufferings. I prayed, "Oh, Jesus, Thou are so kind to us. How slowly Thou dost teach us resignation and detachment whilst Thou didst receive and accept the world in a most cruel way. Thou could not even be dressed to die. How can we compare our resignation toward wayward children who are wrapped in blankets of prayers in Thy arms and pinned with Thy word *Trust* upon Thine own heart? Oh, how can this little trial compare with Thy holy resignation to leave the holy peace in eternity to dwell amongst us? I believe, Beloved Jesus, the pain Thou didst experience to become God-Man for us has never been fully understood nor even given too much thought in finite minds. Oh, Jesus, forgive our stupidity for not more fully thinking of Thee in Thy perfect resignation to leave the Eternal Father and heavenly peace for us who give Thee so little in return."

Resignation now burned its meaning upon my soul as I neared the eleventh station, and my memory seemed to recall these words as if spoken aloud by some kind soul, "To believe in resignation is to act, and to act is to beg of Thee, Jesus, to permit our spirit to be nailed to Thee on the cross of redemption. Permit our bodies to remember always that the weight of body is our living cross, and our spirit is Thee, my God, struggling under the heavy cross and in this desire, Beloved Jesus, we'll believe we are nailed to Thee, with Thee and through Thee for our souls' salvation.

"Jesus, oh my Jesus, Thy cross and my cross is now lifted up. We are on a stairway between earth and Heaven. Permit me to travel onward with Thee, and I'll promise to try to keep my mind in Heaven, my cross (body) at Calvary, and my will as a constant companion beside Thee, my Jesus, in the Blessed Sacrament. And when death enraptures my spirit with Thy love, permit my spirit for a moment to kneel before Thy cross (my body) and burn a vigil light for the world to love better the Stations of the Cross."

My desire seemed to please our Jesus and in reply He said, "My little holy widow for whom you are praying for the gift of joy in resignation toward her son is My loving victim of love. At the holy table, she not only brings Me one chalice (her own soul), but she brings Me a thousand other chalices to receive Me mystically in them for the salvation of souls who have forgotten Me in the many paths to Calvary. My little widow well understands the meaning, 'I die to self each day that others may live.'"

In vision's inner light and understanding, I seemed to watch our little holy widow kneeling before our Jesus near the Communion table. From her heart she took forth her golden chalice glittering with diamonds of love. She lifted it toward our Beloved Jesus, and He smiled upon her offering of love. As she held her chalice aloft to Jesus, I noticed from the cup of the chalice unfolded huge petals, petals like an unfolded rose, huge petals of spun gold and, as each petal unfolded from the cup of the chalice, it resembled another golden chalice, a thousand petals, a thousand chalices of love, all on one stem of love. My soul cried out in prayer before the vision of sublime love, "Oh, chalice of a thousand petals, oh mystical rose of charity living again for us and with us in the body of the holy little widow of love, come dwell with all thy children in the grace of charity, and make us with thee, oh Blessed Mother of God, another mystical rose of love to be redeemers of souls with thee for thy Son."

My Beloved's nearness seemed to leave my soul, as well as the knowledge and nearness of the sleeping child. With my arms mystically raised to our Blessed Mother's shrine, I gave her my little brother's soul to watch and care for until I took him again for a walk to Calvary.

God bless God!

MYSTICAL HUMANITY

Father Frank Reaches for the Mystical Book

Oh, Holy Spirit, our beloved joy in God, Thou hast invited us to seek Thy love, Thy nearness, and Thy consolations through prayer of quiet, which alone touches the heart of God. Tonight I seek Thy consolation of help and understanding to guide my soul, which seems to be shrouded with many doubts and fears as to the deeper meaning, how to fulfill the mission Thou has given me.

Beloved darling of my soul, these quotations are not contradictions nor is the vision from Thy heart, but I will fail to grasp the hidden meaning, and I need Thy holy guidance lest I fail to execute Thy desires. Permit my soul to please Thee, to better understand Thee and the purpose within the mission of my life, Thy Mystical Humanity. To understand, Beloved, the path of my mission would be to say with deepest sincerity, "Not my will be done, but Thine."

The knowledge of our Beloved's love seemed to reverberate through my soul as though it were whispered into my heart. His silent whisperings pierced my heart in a noiseless, woundless way, like a robin's wing cutting the midnight air, leaving neither trace of song nor flight, yet the will understood as did the pathless skylines: the Master hath spoken.

In His silent whisperings, I understood the questions I had asked, and our Beloved answered me in regards to His Mystical Humanity that it was necessary for me to live my chosen vocation with Him as my companion. Loaning Jesus my humanity for Him to govern as well as dwell within would make my life a living prayer, for He was life, living life within me, and my body now dead to me was His living cross, His cross to take to Calvary, and from Calvary to the door to eternal life.

Our Beloved's whisperings taught me my duty in regards to writing His thoughts of inspiration for myself and friends. I was to write His silent wisdom and understanding as though they were love letters from Him to the world.

As I listened in deeper quiet prayer, I heard our Jesus say, "Quiet propagation is the real life leading to eternity. Quiet propagation is noiseless in its quest to touch souls with faith. Quiet propagation is living one's own vocation for the glory of God. Vocation living for God's glory is louder than words. It is a prayer of love to the Eternal Father."

To be hidden from the world, I understood, was to shun all earthly amusements and occasions of sin, searching always to pray, to teach, and to enjoy His friends whom He wishes to share with us. And to make the "chain longer," our Beloved Jesus spoke, "Write My letters to the world through thine own meditations on My Humanity. In thy meditations I'll speak many times to thee for the world to know Me better. As each letter or meditation is read, the chain grows longer. A chain of mediations is My desire, a constant chain without a break, for meditation never ends."

Instantly, in a transport of His joy, I was permitted to see myself as a tiny child standing in a huge library, looking over the many shelves of books. My eyes followed along the top shelf of books. Finally my gaze rested upon a book whose title read *Love Letters through Meditation to the World*.

Oh, Holy Spirit, I knew the book contained our meditations, our way to His perfect life amongst us, His living within us our joys and sorrows—His living, for we are dead to self. We are the rock through which He resurrects daily to show forth His goodness and to again walk among men.

In meditation's prayer and as the tiny child, I desired the book on the shelf more than anything on earth. In it I found a newborn joy, for it told of Jesus, and the meditation's light taught me it contained the world's last devotion, the Mystical Humanity within us. As the tiny child, I tried to reach the book but found myself helpless to reach the shelf. Into the mystical room in the world of meditation walked my earthly father (John Hession). He also tried to reach the book for me but found he was not tall enough. However, he assured me he would try other ways to obtain the book I desired. Then in walked Father Frank Parrish. He seemed taller than usual and, in the light of understanding, I understood he represented the complete Jesuit order. With no effort, Father Frank reached the book and gave it to me to hold. I caressed it and was about to open it when Father Frank spoke these words, "You cannot open the book. They are not finished. When they are finished, I'll open it."

COLORS OF THE UNIVERSE

My weekly confession ended, and with a lightsome heart I left the sacred hall of justice (the confessional). Like anew, my soul seemed to wear as an emblem the kind words from my confessor's lips. Words there placed were never to be erased, for they had touched my soul with new light, hope, and understanding in the tender mercies of God.

Into dark depths of disappointment I had fallen because I had felt disheartened in what I thought were futile efforts and attempts to love Jesus and to have others love Him as the divine Human Friend and God to all. As I walked nearer to God's tabernacle home on the altar, with a prayer of thanksgiving in my heart, I felt our Beloved's embrace of love, and there it seemed I fell asleep in His arms as a tiny child. Asleep in meditation's prayer, I was graced with vision knowledge to understand (in a tiny degree) God's loneliness in His tabernacle prison for us sinners who neglect Him, our silent, willing Prisoner.

While thus praying in thanksgiving for the gift of His most chosen desire (the grace to console Jesus in His loneliness), meditation's whispered breath spoke into my sleeping soul these words, "Little soul in God, remember always with God there is no time."

I found myself as the infant listening to the beating of God's Sacred Heart. Like gentle knocking upon a door, it seemed to be persistent in calm, quiet, and peace, to reverberate through my soul these words, "Plead with man to heed My inspirations."

I answered, "Dear Jesus, I believe through Thy grace, Thy gifts are many and great, and may be gained if we but open the door of our hearts to better heed Thy ever whispering voice and give ourselves to Thee." As my prayer ended, the altar and tabernacle before me faded away into the mist of meditation's time. There, in the midst of heavenly tones of music seen with the spiritual eye (tone as color and blending hues), stood our divine Shepherd clothed in a cope of red and gold over an ivory and blue gown. His sandals were gold and covered with jewels matching in brilliance the tall golden crosier that He carried magnificently in His right hand. As Jesus walked slowly toward the communion rail where I knelt, He sang these words with a delightful air of happiness, "My delights are to be with the children of men."

Bowed in adoration and feeling the nothingness of self, I felt as though I lived for a moment in the blissful quietness of His Heart. I felt and understood within the blissful joy of His love that air, light, and the beautiful mysteries of unfolding time did not heed the calculus of earthly time. In happy nothingness of self, I watched our Jesus in all His human God-Man beauty walk toward the spacious west.

With His hand firmly clasped to the crosier of jewels, His eyes fixed on Heaven's depths, His lips moving in constant prayer, I heard His steady step—walking, walking, walking for our joy into the meaning of time. His every step, so sure and perfect, echoed into my kneeling body, there to breathe great pain to my earthly flesh and my soul, as one in adoration's agony breathed aloud these words, "Oh perfection in Thy holy walk, give us grace to follow in Thy footsteps, there to walk and walk and walk, there to reverberate Thy kindness and perfection to all fellow-men."

Jesus walked on, and the shining light of purity from within the natural tan of His divine features withered and shrank my soul as a tongue of fire curls about a tissue-paper fragment. To my knees I fell and prayed, "Oh, my Jesus, I cannot gaze again upon Thy Holy Face of purity, lest I fall into the sin of presumption and vainness in this great happiness Thou hast given me. I am weak. I am little and I am so afraid my sins do cover me from Thy sight. Oh, Jesus, whilst I gaze towards Thee with closed eyes, please look upon me with Thine eyes of mercy and give me grace to better follow Thee."

As if a cloak of joy were falling upon me, I seemed to gather courage and again opened my eyes to Jesus. His smile of understanding filled my heart to overflowing and I sang aloud in prayer, "Oh, sweet pain, thou are God's reflection in my poor soul, and the pain I feel is the result of His great grace and that grace is God's joyous smile into my heart. Jesus, oh my merciful God, would that I could now become dust beneath Thy holy feet."

With God's gift of grace adding strength to my soul, and with great desire through grace to watch with Him, through Him, and by Him, I seemed to follow into the path of His holy eyes better to gaze upon the world and universe in its hidden beauty as seen only by the eyes of the soul within the nothingness of self hidden in God's majesty.

I heard myself whisper aloud in prayer, "Great Love, give me grace to watch with Thee into the immensity of Thy time and space, remembering all the while it is for Thy delights alone that I learn Thy way better to give souls the knowledge to know Thee better on earth and to enjoy Thee in greater depths forever in Heaven."

There with Jesus in my soul's gaze arose great glittering, towering triangles, reaching in height from earth to Heaven's arch. They seemed to be distinct and set apart in space, like opening pages of a book, with no infringement or shedding of one's light or knowledge upon another page. Each triangle radiated and at the same time held its own color, hundreds of colors, colors to match any shade the earth has ever known. There, color and colors lay in their own beauty, majesty, and mystery, so great as to fill all imaginations to overflowing in God's grace of His immensity.

As I watched the panorama of glory and color with Jesus, I noticed and felt I was completely oblivious to all earthly surroundings, sound, time, and space.

Slowly the huge triangles moved toward me, better to reveal knowledge, love, and joy to those souls hidden in Jesus in the grace of humility and prayer. I adored my Jesus, and in spirit I kissed His feet while the immense triangle in its own color of silver and its million hues slowed to a full stop before me. With Jesus, in silence where brooded eternity, I watched the magnificence of a soul's delight as I ventured into the silver depths within the awesome triangle. In an instant of wisdom and understanding, I was shown every silver ray of light or silver object the earth and all creation had ever witnessed. I loved the light from the flash of silver light in the tiny rain puddle to the rippling waves of lakes, and the mighty sprays of oceans' waves all in immensity caused me to love Jesus more and more, for I understood nothing ever created is ever lost. There, hidden and in profound silence lay everything of silver light, reflection, and purpose to add to His immensity in quiet repose. The magnificent silver light of all spreading dawns throughout the complete universe from the beginning of time until the end of time seemed to signal permission for my soul's joy to become a participant in its enveloping gladness of glory and adoration before its Creator.

Sinking slowly into the exquisite silver depths of all created dawns and their trailing fans of magnificent light, I felt an immersion of happiness throughout my soul, and my soul seemed to pray these words: "Oh, sweet immersion, thy glory in wisdom is soothing, soothing as the tranquilities of a sleeping pool. Oh cover me, beautiful tranquilities of rest, for in thy light I believe I have found my Heaven." In delights added to delights, my soul seemed to fall into a languid sleep as it began to mix and mingle with the now rapidly changing moments of past time, where each dawn and flash of light once existed for souls' delights while they lived on earth. I watched into the great dawns of past time, and they seemed to fall like sheathes of light falling away from great truths of silver outlines that revealed great and mighty empires of earth's past. Solemn, rotating colors of untraveled worlds rose and fell like music in the silver mists of time and then more slowly and in accord with eternal silence in the silver-ordered world. All things seemed to vanish beneath me into the huge drifts of silver clouds. My soul, like a tiny moth in a whirlpool of sheer delight, drifted into even greater delights of revolving cascades of unthought-of light and knowledge. Languishing here and there for my own pleasure, I seemed to travel through mighty fountains, silver-sheened towering mountains, mists, and eternities of ice reflections. I was often reminded of historical possessions and scenes reminiscent of my earthly life, meaning, purpose and accidental truths.

Seeing all this—God's grandeur of pleasure and beauty and magnitude—I realized I loved the grandeur more than my Jesus. Then I realized I had not missed His tender gaze and kindly smile of hope. And again my eyes followed the awful path of beauty, and I was relishing and trying to believe this pleasurable slumber of beauty was the goal and crown of all happiness.

Then, through His tender gaze of mercy, I was awakened to the state of my soul. There lay my soul like a filthy animal covered with sores, breathing in the beauty of time with no heed for God. As my memory tried to recapture in thought my Beloved's Holy Face, I heard the fallen angels calling to me these words, "She is a gift to us through the folly of pleasure. She loves the Heaven for fools." Then all the evil voices seemed to give utterance to the claiming of my soul while my soul and memory, still fixed on the thought of God's Holy Face, battled broodings of terrible confusion. Where was Jesus? Memory, like a vanquishing chieftain, awakened more fully from its sleep and hurriedly searched for the Holy Face of Jesus who, for long moments like an eternity, had been forgotten. Memory, in its hurried search for Jesus, seemed to cling to the desperate moments of fleeting time as a dying soul clings to life. I cried aloud in anguish and grief, for I could not find Jesus even in my memory. "Oh my God, I am alone. I fear I am lost. Oh my God, the power of these immensities find me struck me with fear, and now I feel the protecting robe of these silvered atmospheres, like petals of a rose, unfolding away from me, leaving me alone to be my soul's own judge. Jesus, my God," I cried, "Deliver me from the convictions of sin in pleasure that seem to shout and flare about me." I heard evil voices crying, "You have forgotten God. Your vain solace, the gods of clay in their silvered kingdoms, now glare upon their harvest."

I seemed to pray aloud in fearful sorrow these words, "My God, my God, my sinful soul in its quest for happiness in beauty hath forsaken Thee. I seem to be alone in all created beauty, alone. Oh my Jesus, please find and save me, for I am now slowly sinking into a silvered grave of pending darkness, where black depths emerge to clasp into darkness a fallen soul. Oh my Jesus, only Thee, my God, can find and save me. Jesus, mercy."

With the suddenness of prayer answered through His mercy, I found myself encased in a robe of greater light. I prayed in joyful knowledge, for fear had left when I felt the shroud of mercy through the use of His Holy Name, Jesus. I prayed into the beautiful, returning memory of His Holy Face these words, "Dearly beloved Jesus, for love of us Thou has said, 'I know my own and mine know Me.' My Jesus, my Love, I offer Thee all praise and a hundred million loves in gratitude, for I am Thine because Thou has placed Thy lighted cross upon my soul, the sublime gift of the Living Bread, which now casts its shadow of impenetrable light over darkness and leaves my soul in freedom's golden light above all created and uncreated worlds. Oh, Jesus, would that I could atone for the folly of forgetting Thee, my Jesus, for the beauty of earth and creation. But how can this desire be accomplished, for I am but a lull in nothingness without Thee? Yet I beg to offer Thee my will and all my earthly goodness as a sacrifice to atone for my ingratitude."

As I offered Jesus the gift of my will, I found myself kneeling again beside our Master's feet as He walked again toward the west singing His song, "My delights are to be with the children of men." The great silver triangle moved into space and silence, there to remain forever as His masterpiece of joy, for souls to enjoy who wish to remember for all eternity the likeness of earthly objects which they enjoyed whilst living on earth.

As I listened to His melodious voice, again I felt as one dead in nothingness of self. Then I thought I heard myself praying these words, "Oh, mercy, my Jesus of love, for my soul is weakening. Oh, spiritual love, embrace me, for I am nearing many of Thy great and terrible triangles of color and beauty that may sway the reason of my understanding to forget Thee, my God. Permit me in humility and in Thy grace of understanding to venture into their depths, into their beauty and immensity, but this time all for Thee, my Jesus."

Jesus answered, "Heaven in all its glory will have as it were before its door the spiritualized memories or accidents of earthly thought which one sees now in earthly natural form. All will rest in form, order, and peace from the beginning of creation until the end of time before that mystical door of knowledge, wisdom, and understanding. The beauty of not only the earth but all sister worlds will assemble and rest in this natural, spiritualized setting of My order and purpose for souls to enjoy when they seek joy in reminiscing about earth and its possessions."

My soul shrunk in fear before the oncoming triangle of reddish gold as it swayed in all its shades and hues before me. Words, mortal words cannot begin to tell of its magnificence, its magnitude, its simplicity and peace, as it entered into my soul through the gaze of our Beloved's eyes.

My soul for the moment seemed completely dissolved in all eternities' golden sunsets, tinted clouds, and the gold of stars and reflections of all the universal suns. All the colors of red, reddish gold, and copper the world had ever used were now shown in magnificent delights of joy for Jesus, as though hidden in the joys of sublime adoration and thanksgiving to God for His gifts of beauty to the elements of time. My soul, overcome with joy in the awesomeness of holy beauty, prayed aloud, "Oh, my soul, you are so weak. I am so afraid. Oh, my soul, don't wither and fall away in death through the cause of beauty in God's creation. Oh, my Lord and my God, lift Thy hand in benediction lest I fall. Give me grace to gaze upon Thy creation of magnificence better to gain the grace of knowledge for Thy desire, but all for Thee, my Jesus, and not for my joy."

My soul swooned as though dissolving into the magnificence of holy fire, and I prayed aloud in the greatest of pain, "Take me away. I am afraid. Dissolve me in Thy heart, oh Jesus, but spare me from the fires of Thy creation's heart of beauty. Take me away. Take me away, my Jesus of mercy."

Breathing lighter and resting calmer through His grace of holy benediction in taking me away from the torments of beauty, power, and grandeur in red, I felt an inner peace and joy caressing my soul, and there before me reposed His creation in blue. Slowly its magnificence dawned upon my soul, nearly beyond spiritual control, to watch and behold its awesome depths. For a moment its sheer delights swayed my reason, and I experienced the feeling of total loss of soul, but hurriedly the grace of reason in memory recalled to my soul the thought of our Lord's Holy Face, and there it was no longer a memory but a fixed reality; fear left me for I was enjoying the blue of all creation for His joy, not mine.

My soul cried aloud, "Oh, magnificence in blue in God's creation of joy for souls, thy beauty tantalizes my soul with a longing to fall into your very depths, there to be forgotten. For surely this joy, peace, and solitude must be near the likeness of real Heaven. Oh blue of blue, thy sweetness, thy depths, thy color, all an immersion of joy, seems to hold my heart in a crushing wave of ecstasy, Oh my Jesus, all for Thee."

My soul ventured into the blue world where blossomed a hundred thousand shades of blue. There in twilight depths, a million different worlds in breathtaking depths swung like listless clouds upon the immensities of God's thought. Far below the vision of worlds and cloud, I gazed into endless space where endlessly lapped the heavens' blue seas upon spacious shores of blue sand. The great sea's silent fondness and delight in adoration for its God seemed to caress with gentle fingers (mists and waves) all of God's accidental truths in blue, much like a mother caressing her child.

While watching in meditation's profound sleep, the great drama of perfect silence in the sea's adoration of God, I was given to understand the five mortal senses are *one* and, as I understood, I could actually see perfect rhythm, beautiful silent music, far more beautiful and majestic than tones of earthly hearing. I noticed I was looking and listening at the same time to the sea's swirling currents, and in them I saw reflections of shady nooks and flower beds of earth. The flowers and shady nooks arose in tones as different and intriguing as matchless flower heads. A few tones—as intangible as contemplation—seemed reverberant with children's laughter, which shook a tangled forest with a gentle breeze of love, and from the tangled forest there echoed forth every holy word and thought of every people in all earthly time. Here I was given to understand that nothing God created can be destroyed into a complete finality of nothing. He created our spirit, and that same spirit created words, thoughts, motives, and actions which are in truth our accidental truths, a part of our own personality which shall live forever in God's plan of order.

In the great blue distance, hidden as if veiled in a mist, earth's sorrow sighed amid its great paramount gods. They resembled, to the spiritual eye, earth's bare, jagged cliffs, and from their slopes gushed mountain brooks bubbling with praise, alms, and adoration of aimless denominations in false religions. In the cliff's dark ravines, blue orchids stood as if by proxy to relate a sad, sad story of lost souls, and from the orchids' throats I saw the hurling clouds of once worded words telling of revolt, anger, and vengeful thoughts, while in a swamp the bluebell (the symbol of souls rejecting race) hung, its tinkling song long ceased, and from its nectar flowed the words and thoughts of blasphemies and broken trinities.

While I watched the spiritual life of silence in words of both good and evil, I felt in my soul great feelings of sorrow and joy, and I wished and longed for my own death so that I would cease to add words of anger, hatred, and revenge to the tide of sorrow and sin.

I looked again for the Holy Face of Jesus, and there in the power of memory He smiled His grace of love. Before me arose a magnificent blue, so terribly blue its beauty and power over soul it compelled me to pray, "Hail, most holy Mother, I feel Thy nearness in this, God's accidental[7] creation, for us, through us, and in us."

In the joyful thought and understanding of "Mother," an ocean without a shore came into spiritual view. It tossed its blue-tipped waves higher and higher, creating a sweet chord of music which told and resounded throughout the complete bluish triangle these words: "Blessed are souls whose sins are covered. Blessed are they whom earth's confessors blessed." As I silently repeated this phrase time and time again, it seemed I was watching a beautiful vision of our Blessed Mother's voice rising from the shoreless ocean in praise and thanksgiving for our priests of today. And in vision's knowledge, I was given to understand how each soul's sins confessed in the confessional on earth reverberated into the heavens' blue of blue with tones like mighty trumpets heralding good news to all creation. All confessed sins arose in tones as one perfect rhythm, rising and breaking like a tidal wave of pearls, in their splashing awakening the world to an elevation of understanding of the word, "crucify, crucify," which now echoes and re-echoes in all earth's seas as the real waves break against the earth's shores.

The pearl-breaking waves of rhythm cast their glinting rays like sunshine down into the blue of blue in the center of the huge triangle, there to reveal the one everlasting night of nights, the terrible Crucifixion.

In the distance, upon a crest of earth's twilight, stood a blue cross in shades of evening blue, and upon that cross hung the blue bruised

---

7 In this context, the word *accidental* does not mean "by chance." Accidental creation refers to the radically different world that existed prior to the Original Sin.

Body of Jesus. From each wound and bruise flowed a thinning veil of blood, ever flowing toward earth like endless comets of grace to fill the hearts of blessed penitents.

I watched a world of blessed penitents receiving grace upon grace through the gift of confession. They grew in wisdom and cherished the power of absolution given them by earth's confessors, Christ's ambassadors. As I watched in delight the beautiful grace of wisdom in its way of forgiveness, I suddenly heard great rumblings which touched my soul, and I understood they were discords on earth caused by sin in sad neglect of Jesus in the Blessed Sacrament. Within my soul, I sensed the great pain of loss for myself and friends who neglected Jesus, our silent Prisoner. Earthly pain in my body shattered the vision from my soul's sight, and peace and quiet fell away, dissolving my soul into nothingness before the dimming of one holy, magnificent light.

Meditation's sleep in soul's depths ended, and I seemed to return to Jesus, there to kneel before Him and better listen to Him sing His delightful song, "My delights are to be with the children of men."

As Jesus sang His song, He walked slowly into meditation's path. There beside Him, I prayed these words, "Great love, please give me the grace of perfect detachment, for it will take that grace to leave the beautiful spectrums of green and violet and the many other shades in the great and terrible triangles of beautiful, hidden mystery as a sacrifice of penance for my neglect to Thee, my Jesus, in the Blessed Sacrament. Please give me the grace to remember the vision and understanding in Thy wisdom, the better to relate to friends Thy hidden mystery of love for them when they reach their journey's end. Help me, Jesus, to write them as You would like them written for Thy glory to be better known among men. May Thy glory be glorified through my memory, to write Thy wishes for the benefit of mortal souls who are held beneath the iron rule of prophets who find delight in their earthly strength in teaching a doctrine which embraces the broken Trinity."

My soul in thanksgiving for the granted desire (for He smiled and I understood) adored His sacred Face, and in spirit I followed His holy eyes into the depths of darkness beneath His feet.

Through the black clouds a glittering spear appeared, piercing upwards through the clouds like a lightning streak, there to cross the features of God's Holy Face with its shadow. Our Lord walked on as one in sorrow. Now His glorious features were blurred by the shadow of earthly sin. I cried aloud as if I were crying to the entire world, "Oh, ingratitude of man, you have crossed the light of God from your souls." Then, as if in answer to my call, the depths of Hell answered, and the folly of men's ingratitude sent forth a second spear to cross the first shadow and the vision of the Holy Face was gone, along with all the colors of His masterpiece in the mystery of the hidden triangles, the accidental earth. In vision's view through the spiritual contemplation, the earth appeared bleak and cold, and there in perfect silence on a faraway hill stood a silent cross, and on that cross hung the stilled body of Christ. Then I understood in wisdom's grace of knowledge that, for an instant, I was watching the Crucifixion and from God's eyes wherein he beheld all creatures ever to be born, I sensed that every creature was there present at the foot of the cross.

Every soul seemed to be asking to share in His sufferings, while another, smaller group pleaded to share with Him a complete crucifixion, with Him, through Him, and by Him.

This vision vanished as I watched earth's future generations looking forward into Heaven's heights; there in the spacious heavens, wrapped in winding linens, visible to them alone through eyes of faith, was once again our Sacred Jesus. He was alone and far from His masterpiece of colors, no glowing tan of light now pierced His marble face. His Holy Face, stilled in death, seemed to coax me nearer to His side and there, kneeling beside our Jesus, I was permitted to watch earth's conflict with coiling obstinacy (much like a huge snake) with souls rejecting the grace to love Jesus more in their desire for human respect.

There in vision's intellect, Jesus showed me life eternal through the crystal flaming cross as it slowly formed before His sacred lips, which proved to be the seal of the sepulcher for each and every one who receives the gift of God, the Holy Eucharist. In an infusion of grace, I understood every soul who has received the Blessed Sacrament receives a signal grace upon his or her soul, a grace that to spiritual eyes resembles a crystal of white fire. The cross grows in brightness as sanctifying grace increases. Thus the body is never in darkness, not even in the grave, for the light of the cross pales the noonday sun.

Millions of souls breathed this prayer, as the mystery of the Resurrection cleared before their eyes, "Accidents of bread and wine, please brighten our cross before our lips, the door to our sepulcher and key to the eternal life of God."

Millions of other children prayed thus, "We, Thy children, believe through faith, God in all His wealth, beauty, and power in mercy remains hidden amongst us in the Bread of Heaven. Oh, Bread of eternal life, help us to love Thee more."

My eyes left the peoples of the earth and again found our Lord's sacred Face. There, above the flaming cross of crystal fire before His lips, formed a mist of waving lilies which slowly veiled the holy cross of crystal fire. Through wisdom and knowledge, I was permitted to understand a simple story of the mystery of the great resurrection through the vision of the lilies. There a story unfolded which I am sure every man and child may learn and understand as well as love, if they would but search earth's far-stretched [plains] for just one glimpse of the lilies' creation, especially the tiny lilies of the valley. There one may find them hovering close to the rock of earth, beckoning, coaxing with their incense, every man and child to bend their knees in admiration and love of them. I heard my soul sigh these words in the sight of such fragile beauty, "Look, man, to the existing realms above and hold close to your heart the captured love of simplicity and pure thought from the lilies. Touch the hem of thy God's cloak with the wand of prayer. And, man, as the lilies incensed your path to pursue the bending of your knee, so, too, your prayer in love and adoration paves your way to the King's Highway, the Holy Eucharist."

My soul wept with a delightful peace in the knowledge of the simple resurrection and the story of the lilies in such beautiful simplicity. Thus, learning to love simplicity and from its holy grace I watched another mystery of this fantastic world. Slowly, slowly, mother earth rolled into darkening gloom for earth dwelt in a mood of anguish; anguish because pain for sin now heavily slept in a world of ease. The offering of pain for sin and earth's trials seemed to be a grace of the past.

As I watched the earth in its great minuet design, my soul poured forth this prayer for my people, the Mormons, "Oh, my God and God of love, in Thy tender mercy, save my people. In Thy mercy Thou hast given me the grace of love of reparation for self and friends; now I offer Thee the sacrifice of my meager will in thanksgiving for Thy tender mercy. Remember, Jesus, once I was Thy greatest care. Yes, I was Thy greatest sinner, and Thy tender gaze of mercy did save me.

In Thy holy grace, my soul was permitted to kiss Thy sacred shroud and see, in faith, Thy glorious Self hidden in the lifted Host each day in the holy sacrifice of the Mass. I believe and trust in Thy mercy because I remember Thy holy words to the prophets of old, 'My hand is outstretched still.' Oh, hear my prayer in Thy kindness and grant my sacrifice of my will to be forever dissolved beneath Thy feet, there to be woven in Thy embracing love. Permit my soul in Thee and by Thee and through Thee to glorify God the Father by the repeated song of my people in the days to come when they shall lift their hearts to Jesus in calling for the shroud of Crucifixion in the form of the Living Bread."

As my prayer ended, I watched a mourning dove carrying in its mouth a thousand lilies and winging its way round and round the earth. In the dove's weariness, the lilies fell to cover the earth, and I thought they were lost in the dark clouds forming around the world. But, to my surprise, they were not lost but only lighted the way for one to see the earth more clearly as she swung gently and slowly through and among the troubled clouds. My soul nearly fainted at the wonder of how great God must be for just one of His majestic thoughts to stay the fragile earth from shattering into nothingness.

As the light of God, in and through my understanding, fell upon the earth, the earth resembled a huge mass of moving sand, without a tangible something to hold one grain of sand to another. Beams of God's light pierced through and through the earth revealing hidden wonders, awe-inspiring yes, but the mystery of the grave held my thought above everything else. For there in the sea as well as in the earth were millions of crystal, shining crosses shimmering in beautiful light before each marble face in death, proving again the mystery of individual sepulchers with the key to Heaven, the holy cross and its hidden, divine meaning.

The dead of centuries past now showed in the light of each shimming, crystal cross which mysteriously reposed before each face in death.

My soul cried out in a whisper to Jesus, "Even in death we know no darkness. Now, Beloved Jesus, Thou art teaching me how each body of human race which has partaken of Thy gift, the Blessed Sacrament, is Thy tomb and the shining cross, the symbol of the rock before Thy sepulcher. And only Thee, my God, can move that stone when the divine awakening calls for individual resurrections from tombs."

Jesus answered, "Thou hast learned well in the grace of wisdom. Teach thy friends the new meaning of My human tabernacles, the temple of the Holy Spirit, My chalices, and now My tomb."

My soul felt a sickening sorrow as my vision cleared before a darkening view in the coming ages to come. Oh terrible moment, how can eyes behold the sight, for now all human hearts beat sadly for men in their greed of hate toward Mother Church had waged war against the priests of time, killing them wherever they were found. In vision's eye, I seemed to be watching a crowd of people in a darkened cave, their temperaments noticeably of wild chaos and confusion. And there in the dim flickering of two lighted candles, I noticed an altar, and near that altar a priest was offering prayers for the world. The priest knelt and then arose to raise the Sacred Heart for his own adoration and, as he held his sacred God, the Light of the World, into the heavens, a pistol shot was fired. There lay crumpled at the altar the world's last priest, the world's last prayer, the world's last Blessed Sacrament. In cooling fingers rested the Sacred Host. The noise of the hissing people had ceased. Deathlike calm swept the earth for Jesus Himself, the great High Priest, was finishing the Mass. Millions of holy angels were the worshipers, and they seemed to say, "Truly the gates of Hell did not prevail." While they sang in response to Jesus and his prayers, the Blessed Mother knelt beside her last priest and from his still fingers she lifted the Sacred Host into her hands and offered the Sacred Host to her Son, Jesus. Jesus broke the bread and, as the sound of breaking filled the air, the earth trembled and great earthquakes filled the complete earth.

Our Blessed Mother received from our Lord a part of the Sacred Host, and she seemed to place it into the light of her own heart while Jesus received the remaining particle as a priest in His Communion at Mass. There in our Blessed Mother's heart reposed the glowing fires and radiations of love from the Blessed Sacrament, there to remain always, remain forever, as a remembrance to souls in Heaven that upon this Bread we were once nurtured for life eternal. My heart sang aloud, "Oh, Blessed Mother, thou art our eternal tabernacle and forever and ever; thou dost show forth thy Son's humanity in the Blessed Sacrament. Oh, Queen of the Heavenly and last Sacred Host in creation, we love you now and forever."

Grace from the earth had fled in the symbolic form of a million doves winging their way to God's light. As the last priest breathed his last breath on the altar step, the sun in the heavens hid its light and the moon and stars were no more. People grew afraid, and in terrible fear they searched for the last priest to give them absolution. Now in fear they would turn to God where heretofore He had offered them the ways of love, and they had spurned His call to follow Him.

Hundreds of people, crawling on their hands and knees over one another, tried to reach the stilled form of God's priest. They kissed his cold body. They wept in deepest sorrow. The raised his cold hand and asked God to give him life to make the Sign of the Cross over them in and through the grace of absolution. My soul wept for the poor people, and I realized I was beholding the world's greatest tragedy, the world's greatest moment in sorrow, the world's greatest moment in lamentations and weeping, the world's last moment in time. "Oh, Jesus, mercy, mercy, to these poor souls," is all I could say.

Our Blessed Mother fondly kissed the sacred brow of her last priest and left with the angels to hide her light from the ungrateful children on earth. Jesus turned to the people in the cave, as would our priest turn to bless us in the last blessing in the Mass, and there He stood for a moment looking out over the world. Then His eyes fell to the body of the last priest. He tenderly knelt to the cold body and raised the cold arm; with it He made the sign of the cross in a giving grace for absolutions of thousands of souls. Then, turning to the altar, our Blessed Lord touched one by one the candles and the world was in darkness, silence, and fear, for even Jesus Himself was not there at the altar.

Moments seemed like years, and then in the eastern sky shone a brilliant cloud of silver and with it the sound of a million voices filled the heavens' air with singing and prayer. All on earth knew it was the last day, the last moment, and there, in the light of justice in a cloak hiding our God, the people understood justice and its divine purpose.

As the heavens' light neared the earth, it seemed as though an artist had spread its dew across the canvas of time, covering as if painted in sweet, gentle strokes, death to all earth's creatures (animals) as well as life in nature's gardens. I heard the last call of the mourning dove, the last barking dog, and the last tone of a purring kitten. Across my eyes touched the last breath of pines. The vision of splashing brooks and rivers ended. Water stood still and the light of fireflies dimmed and died, as did the soothing glow of summer nights, and I understood I was bidding goodbye to all that creatures love.

All faded as the Artist's invisible brush touched upon all the earth. That death was beautiful and pleasing but, in the heavens as they had never looked before in all created time, the sight was unthinkable, awesome, and terrifying, for out of the silver cloud hurled great waves of lightning streaks toward the earth, piercing the earth and taking her out of the course of time. There into space fell mother earth and, in her fall, all things were swept from her surface, leaving the earth clean and polished. Just sea and land remained. The little earth seemed to be fighting for its last existence, as it plunged into momentary climatic changes and swung here and there far off its course. I watched the sea in its great unrest, climbing, reaching, soaring, throwing sprays to heights heretofore unknown, only to return in battering waves to lash the earth while it still fell into space, like a feather rides the eastern gale.

Finally, the earth seemed to be captured and stilled in a mist of translucent folds of clouds and there, in hushed, trembling silence solemn as death, mother earth, as gentle as a caressing linnet, graciously parted the tapestry of death to reveal her precious cargo, the hidden crosses, both bright in the light of faith as well as dimmed through venial sin. Other crosses glistened in the effects of charred sin, all buried since God's will breathed the breath of life into the clay shells of Adam and Eve.

From the spacious silver cloud were heard magnetic voices calling, it seemed, for individual souls. The clearness of tones seemed to lightly touch all substance in earth's dust and, in response to the call from death, all marble faces beneath the shining crosses beamed with light and color. They moved. They turned. They smiled in the shroud of the grave, body and soul at last reunited from a world of separation by death. In tones of joy that filled all space with raptures of happiness, souls grasped the shining key of light before them and arose from the grave into the far heavens, there to dissolve into the Beatific Vision.

As the last glorious, reunited body arose from its grave and souls took with them all the light in the world (their cross of His light), earth seemed dark and alone, with only a twilight light of coldness as a shroud for the millions who were left as though still sleeping in the grave. They were alone and without light, for the true souls of His light had fled before them into the light of God.

With the gift of understanding, my soul seemed to pray aloud these words to the sleeping millions, "Oh, souls in sins of neglect (those souls who spurned the Blessed Sacrament's grace), your darkened shroud means a slow ascension, for thou must follow the light of the holy saints now risen before thee. In their light and charity, thou art saved forever and forever must be content to enjoy though them the raptures of their joy and light through eternal justice, for only those souls who have partaken of the Blessed Sacrament are allowed to be dissolved in God. For Jesus said, 'Except you eat of My Flesh and drink of My Blood, you cannot enter into the Kingdom of Heaven.' And so, everlasting souls of lesser light, thou must forever gaze upon God through His saints rather than enter into God."

After the second slow ascension of dimmed souls (for there were many degrees in this slow ascension) in flight to God in the light of holy saints, I watched other bodies remaining in the dust of earth. They were in numbers beyond counting. There they lay in the ugly brown shroud of sin resembling crawling worms in the earth. Their awakening convulsed the earth and mother earth expelled them and threw their rebellious bodies down into the center of the earth (Hell). They were hideously disfigured from grievous sin. Many other bodies in their slower crawling from the grave were slimy and soft. Others were swollen as from poison gas, far too repulsive for earth to hold any longer. Poor souls, they clamored to arise and found the scriptures told no lie, for they found no life in them, for life is to know and worship God. Their lamps (or crosses) were charred through following the pursuit of the seven virgins who, in slothfulness of mind, thought of God and then drank to God a toast of hate, thus shattering the marble of their hearts to pierce their God with ingratitude. These same souls in earth's great drama had loved and lived the philosophy, "Let's eat, drink, and be merry, for tomorrow we shall die." I watched them with countless others writhe and roll in torments beneath their charred and blackened cross which once had shown with the brilliance of God's greatest saints. Their only desire now was to dash themselves upon mother earth, there to leave a scar of hate and revenge, but mother earth cast them with their followers from her heart into the beckoning flames of Hell—as one would cast with great relief a crown of thorns. As the last hideous creature toppled into Hell's dark caverns, I was given to understand that through God's mercy their needs, memory, and deeds become oblivious to the souls of saints in Heaven.

The oceans' former wild unrest slowly gained in momentum and again tossed furious waves, only to fall from earth in unbelievable haste into the vanishing flames of Hell. The oceans' fall into Hell caused a roar and hissing no mortal words can tell, only to return in quietness, peace, and beauty in the form of great steam arms and mists surrounding the earth, now resembling a great host in the hands of a priest.

Every arm of steam seemed to separate into great fingers covered with jewels in splendors of vapors. Slowly these great jeweled fingers surrounded and dissolved the earth in their ascension and carried every particle of earthly dust to find its place in the garden of color triangles, there to rest in sweet silence before the gates of Heaven.

"Jesus," I sighed, as the holy vision dimmed away, "Have mercy on the souls who reject Thy grace of love and conversion. Help me with Thy grace of understanding and trust to write the vision and knowledge Thou hast entrusted to me for mortal souls to use better to gain true love of Thee. My soul gives Thee thanks for this great trust. In that trust, I believe Thou will help me write the knowledge for souls to use as a stepping stone to love Thee more and, dear God, please permit this knowledge through Thy grace to awaken a soul to Thee as he lingers near the brink of Hell."

My soul cried out as Jesus smiled upon my nothingness, "Oh, my Jesus, Thy lingering smile, I cannot part with Thee. Would that I could this moment choose death to go with Thee. Oh, Jesus, have mercy on my frailty and fear about the mission Thou has entrusted to me. Please help me with Thy grace. Imprint Thy holy smile upon my memory as a pledge of trust in Thee. Oh, Jesus, what can I do for Thee?"

Jesus smiled and with a slight bow He said, "You may give Me your eyes. Through earthly eyes I love to live again. Through your eyes, I'll gaze into souls, there to imprint My love, My will, My trust they will follow Me."

MARRIAGE

My soul sped away into threading depths of prayer, where prayer is soundless and where one's own heartbeat seems like softly treading footsteps upon the sands of time. There, in mediation's silence, I found myself imprisoned in prayer, imprisoned in light as though my soul wore a shroud of fire, better to blend with the great golden sea of fire which glistened before me. Within the great sea's depths of solitude, I felt the joys of God's redeeming love piercing my heart with knowledge of our Lord's nearness to my soul in His Humanity.

There suddenly stood Jesus before me arrayed in all His splendor as Christ the King. As I knelt before Him, I understood and felt there was nothing on earth with meaning, gain, or purpose unless all was offered through the motive of love to the Eternal Father through Jesus.

Jesus smiled and raised His hand in blessing over me and said, "Why dost thou keep Me waiting for thy visits? Fear not the cloud nor unfathomable sea of golden light. It is but a venture into My heart. The earthly fear which you feel and recognize is for thy humility, for only in humility will thou climb the steps to perfection which I shall teach thee for thy friends and self, better for all to know Me in My Humanity."

My soul cried aloud, "Teach me, Jesus, my Beloved, how to give the knowledge of Thy Humanity to the world. Teach me the simple way to Thee through sensible application in a quest to mortify the senses, better to follow Thee in Thy steps of perfection. Especially instruct me in Thy wishes for my friends who have chosen the marriage sacrament to please Thee."

Jesus answered, "Marriage is oneness of two souls; oneness as I am One with the Eternal Father. The Eternal Father's will is My will. A husband is like unto My priests. His home is a mystical altar; his wife his chalice. When I look into a husband's soul in death, he must give Me an account of his stewardship, faithfulness, care, and devotion to his wife, for has she not given herself completely to his care? A wife's salvation is through her marriage vows, thus giving her husband his rightful honor as head of the house and its lawmaker for all who dwell therein. A wife following this way of submission to her own will travels with joy and little grief into the steps of perfection. Through a wife's humble submission to her husband's will and cheerfulness in all suffering I allow her, she is then graced to carry the mystical cross to Calvary with Me. Thus, in charity and oneness in spirit through marriage, she leads the way to perfection for two souls (husband and wife) in oneness of spirit.

"The wrath of a just God is terrible when He beholds an altar alone or a chalice alone through cruelty, selfishness, and unwilling submission to vows. When a soul must walk alone to perfection through broken vows one to another (through no fault of the one seeking perfection), that soul is indeed a martyr in the eyes of God. Great and grave are the responsibilities of either soul who breaks My chalice or soils My altar through selfishness, jealousy, anger, and pride when in death they stands before Me.

"I desire for those in the sacrament of marriage to receive Me often. In that holy moment, I long to commune with them and, when I speak, it will be of love, for I have said, 'Love one another.' Then I would remind them of the solemn occasion and gift which I have just given them, the use and power of My holy cross. With and through My priest in the Mass, they have written My signature, the cross, upon their foreheads, lips, and hearts. Then all through the day, they sign My signature to their thoughts, words, and deeds, either good or bad, and all these things I must defend before the Eternal Father, for there affixed is My holy cross. Teach My children to be more careful with the use of the signature, My cross.

"When evening shadow find its course over My mystical altar and chalice (husband and wife), oh husband and honored guest to thy chalice, kneel with her in the shroud of My love and retrace the path of tongues and will throughout the day. Let not sleep overtake thee if thou hast made a cross too heavy to bear for those who must obey you. Let not sleep overtake thee if angry and impatient words were spoken. Humble thy selves one to another in My sight and thus remain in Me as little children, and Christlike thou shalt become.

"In such humility of souls, I often speak these words: Have you tried to make your voice like Mine, gentle and mild? Before answering a curt question, did you ask Me how would I have answered it? Did you know, little soul, when you spoke in anger and impatience, you caused Me to follow you? No, you did not follow Me. Anger and impatience are the result of pride, anger because feelings were trod upon.

You raised your voice because of pride. You wished to show authority whilst all the time you are very little. Have I not said, the master must not be above his servant? And all this impatience, pride, and anger I must defend, watch, and listen to by the hour, for there affixed is My signature, the cross, and you have promised to give Me your memory, understanding, and will. In other words, you loaned Me your body for the day, better for me to relive My life again on earth in you.

"Theory and knowledge must be put into practice. Subdue the five senses little by little and become a master of thine own self. Soul and body must act together. Faith without works is dead, as works without faith are dead."

My soul prayed, "Oh, Jesus, teach me a simple method of application, better for myself and friends to practice when one falls through anger and impatience."

Jesus answered, "My little way never fails if souls diligently apply My simple rules of mortification with heroic fidelity for self-discipline and for love of Me. When tongues are guilty of angry words, and if anger has perplexed a soul, purchase for that soul a ten-cent gift and present that gift without a word of explanation, better to mortify thyself in humility and better to teach thine own self the cheapness of anger and the cheapness of thine own self, using My signature without a word or thought or explanation to Me. If souls become angry with a public servant and if they have raised their voice in authority, present thy gift before Me in the Blessed Sacrament."

Again Jesus blessed me and there, before my eyes, dimmed the great golden sea. How drab and uninviting the earth appeared to me. Yet I felt the strange nearness of Jesus and, in His nearness, I trusted He would refresh my poor memory with the instructions He had given my soul for the good of souls who would dare to follow Him in the path of perfection whilst they still live on earth.

OUR LORD'S ONE-HOUR VACATION
INTO THE WORLD

As I knelt before our Jesus in the Blessed Sacrament, I prayed to Him with this thought of gratitude, "What can I do for Thee, my Jesus?

How well I know and realize I am nothing, and Thou dost need nothing I can give or do for Thee. Yet I trust in Thy understanding and mercy toward little souls and, in that trust, my Jesus, I ask again, what can I do for Thee?"

I heard His kind and gentle voice answering, "Would you mind taking Me with you for a walk into the outside world, better for Me to see through your eyes and soul the sunshine, flowers, friends, and homes, and perhaps I'll hear children's laughter. It is always a joy to me. This would give Me an hour's holiday, and through our walk together I'll teach you many new thoughts for your book on steps to perfection to God. This book should be named *Knowing Christ in the Light of Modern Wisdom.*"

Instantly it seemed as though in spirit I was transported with Jesus to another city resembling the one in which I live. Yet I did not recognize the homes, the people, or the streets. Near my side in His Humanity silently walked our Jesus, dressed in a light tan-colored dress and flowing cape of a darker matching color.

Our first stop in His hour's vacation was near a corner where a young boys' football game was in progress. Jesus was enthused and smiled approval many times over the skill and fortitude the young boys exhibited in the harmony of order, as they understood and played difficult codes and numbers which governed the game. Once, as the football sped towards us, Jesus jumped and raised His hand as though to catch it, but a tiny lad intervened and made the catch, bringing a hero's smile to the child's happy face as well as a smile of joy to Jesus.

From round the lad's neck jingled a tone of medals, and Jesus spoke in His silent way, "This boy is wearing My Mother's scapular medal, thus bringing to his aid many of My Mother's angels. In fact, this boy keeps many angels busy, for he is constantly calling on My Mother to catch the ball. Even though she never plays football, she orders her angels to do so, thus giving pleasure to children in their desires as well as affording pleasure for the angels who are earth's greatest cheerleaders. In these games, My angels take sides and the joys in Heaven are very great over a football game when My angels are invited. And you may be sure there are few, if any, games nowadays where the angels are not invited, for they are invited through My Mother's scapular medal worn by the players. That medal is the ticket for choirs of angels through My Mother to many such events on earth. She is the Mother of joy in Heaven and on earth. She forms with her kindness an indestructible bridge (the intercession of the saints), thus giving praise and glory to God forever and ever."

We left the field of fun and walked along the way until we were in view of a well-kept little home. A young mother was calling her children from play. Her voice was calm and gentle with a Christlike mildness that commanded respect and obedience. Our invisible Jesus raised His hand in blessing over the young mother and her precious five children who flocked toward her in joyful laughter. Jesus said to me as He blessed her, "She is a courageous soul. I love her dearly. She takes good care of My little ones in such a way of love that My Mother would entrust Me in My infancy to her care. Often when this little woman rocks her children to sleep at night, she tries to imagine in meditation's way of prayer that she is cuddling Me in My infancy, closer to her heart than her own child. She apologizes for not having more time for prayer. Yet I say this kind of prayer, for it is prayer of application while meditation on My life, thus applying and seeing Me in all things. Often when she rocks her child thus thinking of Me, it is I in disguise whom she is rocking for My Mother two thousand years ago, for with and in God there is no time. For such souls as these, I love to play the role of an obliging God, and so with Me such souls actually live with Me two thousand years ago. It is in those thoughts of meditation with application, even in little things, that I pour out My graces for all families."

"The father, too, is kind and gentle and well understands his chosen vocation in the sacrament of marriage. Often, on his way home from work, he meditates in a most holy way about his family representing special friends to Me and My Mother. Often he pretends his family is giving a party for Me in My childhood, and he must hurry home and take his place as careful watcher, lest perhaps something is wanting which he might do for the success of the party. Thus, in his holy thought for a moment reliving My life in him, I pour out My graces of love, joy, and devotion upon him. Thus he earns graces to make his home joyous, his wife more in the likeness of My Mother, and his children obedient adorers of parent and God."

78

In the eyes and wisdom of Jesus, I was permitted to watch this holy family in evening prayers. They all knelt before a lighted candle flickering its little beams across the Sacred Heart picture enshrined in their main living room. Jesus was indeed the real guest of honor in His rightful place, the real living room in a home.

Jesus spoke, "Blessed are the families who thus give Me the honored place. I dislike being honored in bedrooms and dark corners. I am not ashamed of My creatures nor should they be ashamed of Me. Little do My creatures think or know that My picture with its promises represents Me in the home as guest. I could ask souls who thus hide me away, should I chance to knock at thy door, would you usher Me into your bedroom or some dark corner? No, they would offer Me the best. Even though I am a silent God to many souls, nevertheless I am real, and I know when I am honored and loved above all else in the world. Would that I could tell this blessed family that on holidays when they set a place for Me at table, truly I am there. The chair is not vacant. I'm enjoying every moment in the hearts so rare."

As we walked on down the street, angry voices of women struck our ears. We neared the troubled scene where stood two women, each on her own side of a little, white fence, hurling to one another bitter words of hatred and cursing, all because one another's children had failed to remove sticks and papers from the other's lawn, no doubt thrown there in play or disrespect for property.

Jesus spoke, "How sad. Little do they realize a lawn and its care are not worth the destruction of a soul through anger and unkindness, for charity is kind. Charity is patient. Charity is love for one another."

As angry words continued, the children as spectators listened attentively. It was all so amusing to them. Yet what a terrible lesson in parent conduct to give those children. There before their children's eyes, the mothers threw away priceless gifts: respect, composure, calmness, and gentleness which should be a glistening spiritual gown worn by all mothers and one which should be kept unspotted before the world and especially little children. As the minutes passed, the war of women's tongues grew stronger and stronger, while all the time, little children's souls were scorched and withered by the blistering rays of evil which compassed the mothers' souls. Little children's souls were scandalized, bruised, and made to do evil in thought and gesture because of the mothers' example in the role of motherhood.

Jesus spoke with sadness into the depths of my heart, "Woe unto mothers and fathers who scandalize even one of My little ones."

Through the eyes of Jesus, I was permitted to watch one mother walk briskly into her home, then into her bedroom where hung the Sacred Heart picture. There she knelt before her God's picture and, in anger, asked Jesus to curse the neighbor woman and her children. Then to make the petition stronger, she with her tiny children offered a Hail Mary prayer to hurry its answer. As they left the room, one little boy reached for his mother's hand as if to console her and said, "Jesus will fix her; won't He, Mama?"

Our Jesus walked on down the street and, in a sad tone of voice, He said, "My little lambs are so tender, so impressionable, so easily taught in anger. How poor that mother is, how destitute and how accountable that father is who permits his wife such freedom. Is not her will his? Thus she is acting in his name as well as Mine in the use of My holy cross. Did they not pledge themselves in oneness of self in the sacrament of marriage? How forsaken will their day be when they face justice and give an account of their giving scandal to My little ones, thus teaching them to believe I am a hateful, revengeful, and unmerciful God, rather than a God of mercy, love, and devotion to My creatures."

Into a beautiful country lane we slowly walked together and prayed for the needs of souls in the sacrament of marriage. The country lane's shaded nooks and high, arched pepper trees with clinging vines gave an atmosphere of peace, quiet, and love. We stopped at a low hedge to watch a tiny old lady in her field of flowers. She seemed to embrace each one in a gesture of awe and love. I noticed her flowers were most beautiful in their profusion of color.

Jesus said, "She lives in solitude, better to live and love the sublime vocation I have chosen for her, and that vocation is holy widowhood. She is the symbol of many souls thus chosen. The pattern of flowers in her garden is too a symbol in her way of life. She has learned through patience to come to Me through little ways of love along with doing little acts of work in meditation for love of Me. In her garden there is represented in flowers and shrubs a symbol of her friends either living or dead. This garden represents her world and, in her own little world with Me her companion, she tends to the spiritual needs of her friends by caring for the flowers and offering each bud and new leaf for the needs of friends, or for acts of love to be applied to souls on earth or in Purgatory.

"Over yonder by the outside fence, she has planted shrubs and flowers of a more hardy type, a type which takes little care. They represent to her the friends for whom in life she cared little, yet in the charity of love in her little world she cares for and loves them all. Her chosen flowers, frail and exquisite (friends), she has planted near the center of her garden where she cares for and watches them by the hour."

I noticed a weed here and there in the exquisite beautiful garden. With no question on my part, Jesus gave the answer, "When My dear little lady finds a weed, she meekly prays, 'Dear Lord, Thou art showing me my sins again in the form of ugly weeds in my garden. Thou art kind though not to tell me which one this one represents and so, dear Lord, as I pull this weed from my garden, please remove its roots from my soul, thus leaving the garden of my heart free from weeds, for Thy greater glory and honor.'"

Suddenly we were before the tabernacle home. Jesus was no longer beside me, but deep down within my heart, I heard His kind voice speaking these words, "Little soul in My love, I thank thee for the hour's vacation into the world. The hour has given Me many joys. We have looked upon sadness, too, but the joys overweighed the sinfulness in men. Now for a word of advice for your book, Steps to Perfection for Jesus, always remember I am listening to every word My creatures speak, either good or bad. Now try this for a test each night. Would you blush for shame if I read aloud to you every word thou has spoken throughout the day using thy own tones and gestures? If thou, oh soul, can answer truthfully that thou couldst listen without the blush of shame, then thou art a holy soul in the eyes of God. Resolve each day to watch thy tongue, and in meditation's quiet hour, pretend I am reading thy day's words back to thee for correction, joy, and peace. Thou wilt have little trouble if, when talking to other souls, thou dost try to remember I am listening and then, when thou doest govern thyself always, pretend to talk to Me over My little back fence, the communion rail, and thou wilt have eternal joy. I will plant thee as a rare and choice flower in the center of My heart."

SPIRITUAL NIGHT OF THE SOUL

Oh night of the soul, thou art hard to bear. Thou art invisible, yet as close as a friend. I know it is necessary for my humility and nothing-ness of self to acknowledge thy nearness when thou dost visit me with thy spiritual cloud of darkness, doubts, and fears. Yes, necessary in my climb to Jesus, for through thy powers over my weak nature, better do I learn of my own spiritual weakness and human littleness when Jesus draws away from me for even a little while.

Now that thou are there, oh invisible personalities of evil, I am deter-mined, with the grace of God, to learn a lesson from thee rather than to allow thy powers to affix a question in my mind against the mercies of God. For well I know the shroud of a spiritual night. Often it leaves its mark of questions and disquietude in a soul.

And now in this dreadful hour, better to test my faithfulness and courage for God's glory, I command you, oh personalities of evil, through the holy name of Jesus and the sign of His cross, to show yourselves and speak to me as though you were visible souls.

In meditation's gift of light and understanding, I watched a person dressed in black moving slowly about my room. Aged and bent was he, and lowly he laughed and muttered strange words of praise to himself. As I gazed upon his weak, bent form, I understood he was the spirit of Depression, the spirit often referred to by our priests as the parader of earth seeking souls whom he may devour. His very presence seemed to still my heart, and I understood I was face to face with Depression's invisible personalities: irritability, coarse talk, and lack of respect.

Across the room from Depression sat Self-Pity like a sniveling old woman, hidden and bent in her cloak of darkness. Her ugliness was dreadful and terrifying to the mortal eye. Her mouth was posed into a hideous pout and, when she smiled, great white fang teeth glowed with a greenish, foam-like light.

I spoke with a tone of scorn as I walked toward her, "Oh, how revolting and sad thou dost seem, little woman of awful power. Truly thou are sharply etched with bitterness of tongue as you sit idly by in the detestable glory you call your own. Why even the very look is self-pity, but oh, thy tongue is a consuming fire of jealousy, a devouring fire on whomsoever it may touch. God is merciful to us in not allowing thy true image to transform into life amongst us. I detest thy leprous tongue."

Near the form of Self-Pity stood another form clothed in black rags, and I asked, "Who are thou?"

A thin voice answered, "I am Wonder-Worker Tears. I confess since thou has commanded me to talk through the power of the Master's name, I hate myself. I am unkind and unfair to souls on earth."

As she thus told the truth, my indignation rose against her unfairness and I addressed her in scorn, "Oh thou art the lavish solace and ruination of women who live in little faith and trust in God. To gain thy purpose, oh Wonder-Worker Tears, thou are most lavish with women who use tears as a means to accomplish an injustice both to neighbor and nation. And to a few women, thou art a god. Poor indeed are they who possess little courage and fortitude to fight against thee. Little do women realize the powerful weapon they possess through obedience and submission to authority. Obedience and submission would drive you from them."

Wonder-Worker Tears answered, "Do not tell them of their powers. Women are the most vicious fighters when they rise in indignation against foolish tears."

Alone I stood, viewing my three visitors and I said, "Why, oh visitors of evil from the invisible, dost thou visit me?"

Depression spoke, "We visit those souls who invite us by their diminishing light of grace. We constantly live in hope to receive an invitation from those who know and love God, for through them we receive a special delight to roam through their souls of diminishing light of God's graces. We tire of souls who live in habitual darkness. God's graces withdrew from you. We knew not why unless it was through thine own folly of sin. Had we know the diminishing light was God's withdrawal to test thy skill and fortitude in thy nothingness of self against us, and had we known the step thou hast taken to expose us to the world, we would not have entered into thy soul of peace with God. Release us, please, we beg thee, for through the power of God's holy Name, we are suffering the most dreadful torments of the damned through the knowledge that we are at last going to be exposed to the world."

With voices of anguish and terrible suffering, Self-Pity and Wonder-Worker Tears cried aloud to me as though to ridicule me in these words, "We are the earth's tormentors. We love to find lamenters, woe-seekers, and pity-keepers. And, as earth's chief tormentors, we strive to please our friend, Depression. For him, as you would for thy God, we raise our banner of tears over poor, weak souls. Then we mock them and scold them and finally, when souls fall into earthly tears of woe, we know we have won another soul."

In a scornful voice I answered them, "What dost thou do upon seeing souls weep before a crucifix in sorrow for sins as they leave the confessionals, and what dost thou do when souls weep in joy over God's mercy to sinners?"

Self-Pity answered, "On those souls we dare not gaze. Their light and power burns us."

Then I asked Wonder-Worker Tears, "And what dost thou do when you have caused a soul to weep to gain its will against justice and authority?" And Wonder-Worker Tears answered, "I silently draw back the invisible curtain of Hell," and as she made the gesture, there before me stood her brother, Despair, all aglow in his robes dripping with blood.

Wonder-Worker Tears continued, "He wears long gauntlets, for his touch would burn you to a crisp, and he whispers his commands to us, for his breath would scorch you. With Despair's promptings, we coax your mind into the haunts of past forgiven sins. We delight to attack the confessional, you know," and, with these words, she laughed gleefully.

She continued, "Then, over and over, we repeat thy forgiven sins, and poor souls mull them over and over again. And each time they find new excuses for those forgiven sins; thus trying to excuse sin, they become tired, cross, and irritable, and then we turn them over to sister Curiosity, who loves the scrupulous, and then her way of mind fatigue lulls them to sleep because Depression has visited too long a time."

My soul felt exhausted at such truths and, in fear and trembling, I fell to my knees and cried aloud in prayer, "Oh, Jesus, have mercy on my weak soul. I'm tired and I fear Depression's power upon my soul, for I am nothing without Thee. Come quickly, my Jesus, and take up Thy abode within the kingdom within of my heart and there cast away this dreadful night of the soul. I am weak and weaker still because Thou dost seem so far away."

Then, remembering in littleness of forgetfulness, I hurriedly called on the holy name of Jesus and, one by one, the hideous souls departed into their own world of invisible darkness. And there stood Jesus before me, bathed in His smile of all-loving and merciful kindness, and Jesus spoke as though He were addressing all His friends, "Oh, children of My heart, when worries assail thee, why dost thou not raise thy banner of trust with My name inscribed thereon to save thee from such evils of Depression and Despair? I say to thee, when the monster of Depression brings to light thy forgiven sins, simply remember thou has given them to Me and, through thy penance, I am glorifying them for you, for thy delight when thou dost die in My arms. Would you give a friend a gift, either great or small in value, and then constantly ask him to return it for thy every whim? Why, then, dost thou keep asking Me to return the gifts which you have given Me for safekeeping and for thy own glory through the confessional? Do you not trust Me?

"Remember the story of Saint Jerome. He gave Me everything in his life but his sins. It was most difficult for him to surrender his sins to Me without worry, as difficult as a child parting with a loved toy. Saint Jerome's sorrowing soul and tired body—the result of worry and mistrust over forgiven sin—thus caused him to give Me less praise and glory through trust. I ventured near his heart and asked, 'Jerome, Jerome, thou hast given Me everything in your life but your sins. Where are they?' Oh, children of My heart, remember this. To give Me thy gifts completely in the spirit of charity is to forget what thou hast given Me. This way of life in perfect trust enables souls to live for today, to remember and practice well the lessons I give each soul every day."

My soul still kneeling before Jesus asked Him for a lesson which I would be permitted to remember, better to give myself and friends another little step in the path to perfection through daily helps in and through application and mortification.

Jesus answered, "Let us watch and see," and there before me on the floor mused a cat, playing with a dead mouse. Rolling and rolling over and over again twisted and turned the dead mouse and the cat. The cat appeared well-fed. Apparently it had no desire to eat the dead mouse.

After much play, weary and fatigued, the cat lay down to sleep with the mouse beneath its paw, better as a reminder when it woke to begin all over again its useless play.

In God's graces of wisdom and understanding, I seemed to understand the little drama before me in its symbolic meaning, and I asked Jesus, "Why do we roll the mouse, or in its symbolic meaning, play with our dead and forgiven sins until we are in a state of fatigue?"

Jesus answered, "It is only the animal nature in you or, in other words, the cat in you which loves to mull dead mice. I say to all My friends, arise and clothe yourself in My expression and personality, better to overcome the animal nature in you by application of trust and prayer in Me."

Jesus continued, "You, little soul, have asked Me for a lesson on simple application, better to overcome this grave fault in the world today. Very well, when thou dost find thyself playing and rolling a dead mouse (thy forgiven sins), kneel before Me and say, 'I'm sorry, Jesus. Surely I have played before Thy kingdom today in the likeness of a cat amusing myself with a dead mouse. Help me to be brave and courageous as Thou would have me.'"

I knelt in deepest sorrow for there before me, as though upon a loom, wove a pattern of my life with gold and black threads. The blackness proved to me to represent the hours, yes, the days, when I lacked trust. I was certainly a cat many moments a day.

"Oh, Jesus," my soul pleaded, "Help me to be courageous. Help me to remember this great drama, better for myself and for my friends to learn steps to perfection of self to Thee."

CHRISTMAS EVE

The long vigil of Advent was about over. Yet my great anticipation either to see our Jesus or feel His sublime nearness to my soul made me feel my utter unworthiness. At times the tender desire to see Jesus was extinguished by a flicker of fear—fear I had not lived through the vigil of Advent season in cheerful willingness and submission as the Master would have me live, better to learn detachment from self-will.

At three o'clock on Christmas morning, I knelt in fear and trembling, for my soul was beginning to feel our Lord's nearness. Suddenly, in a rapture of love, I felt the caress of Jesus (or spiritual embrace of love) which alone captivates the soul with interior peace and love. I felt as though his gift to me this Christmas was the grace of greater detachment from friends and the pleasures of the world.

In the shroud of His embrace of love, yet not seeing Jesus, I gazed upon a realm of semidarkness in God's immensities, where space and time as known to the finite senses do not exist. From those realms of darkness, I watched our Blessed Mother caressing in her arms my large crucifix. Slowly and with great tenderness, she caressed the cross and, with languishing delight, she kissed the Sacred Heart. Each time our Blessed Mother kissed the symbol of her Son's Sacred Heart, there arose from the crucifix a beautiful red rose. Silently, it rose toward the far eastern sky as though it had wings of a dove clothed in light from the flaming love of the Holy Spirit. The eastern sky was now a sheen of dazzling brilliance, a dawn of exquisite bliss and peace, a grandeur the likeness of which—even in its least beauty—finite mind would not dare to conceive in the world of imagination. The first red rose, sheathed in brilliant fire, disappeared into the dazzling dawn, only to be followed by a hundred other roses as if they were to form a path for my spiritual eyes, which seemed blinded by the splendor of light. My eyes, following the constant flow of the roses, accustomed themselves to the light of transcending joy, and there in a wide path leading as though from Heaven to earth stood three beautiful horses. Our Lord, dressed in white bishop's robes and with a long crosier covered with jewels in His hand, was seated on the center white horse. To His right was Saint Aloysius seated on a black horse, and in his hand he carried three golden banners whose inscription read, *Verbo espos*—(the rest of the inscription I do not remember).

To our Lord's left, on a huge grey horse, rode an angel clothed in all the silver hues of the eastern sky. The three riders slowly rode toward earth and, as they journeyed, I noticed the flaming red roses were hovering in mid-air over our Lord. Slowly the petals separated from the stems and showered over our Lord as gentle rain. As they fell, our Lord picked one petal from the air and gently placed it into His white sash near His Heart.

It was then I realized I was somehow hidden and transfixed in that tiny rose petal near our Savior's Heart. There, as nothing within nothing, I listened to His Heart and, as I listened to Its perfect timing, I was permitted to see the glow of heavenly light from the sacred Little White Host hidden within the dim outline of His Heart of earthly flesh. My soul cried aloud, "Oh Sacrament most holy, oh Sacrament divine, Thou art the Heart of the universe. Thou art the living Heart on earth. Thou art the living Heart of Thy visible Church on earth."

In an ecstasy of love, in the joyous knowledge of the living Heart in the Blessed Sacrament, it seemed I understood that our Jesus was riding into the country of India. There in the path of Jesus knelt hundreds of adorers and, in their souls' knowledge, I was given to understand they well knew the deeper meaning of the Blessed Sacrament as God indwelling within them as their King and personal guide on earth.

Soon I understood we were in the land of China, where hundreds adored our King in His Humanity within themselves, seeking always to give Him freedom through their body as though He lived as He had after the Resurrection. Hundreds of souls, better to please our Jesus on His birthday, adored Him tenderly as the Holy Infant within themselves after receiving the Little White Host.

As we rode through India and China, our Lord asked Saint Aloysius to plant a banner in each country. I understood our Lord was pleased with the personal devotion which the people of India and China offered Him. As we rode toward America, I heard our Blessed Lord telling Saint Aloysius about my desire for the freedom of India. I realized our Lord was going to do something about my secret desire. Then, as if to please me, Jesus with Saint Aloysius and the holy angel rode through the streets of Utah. It was a very sad welcome and greeting which our Lord received from a few worshipers who understood His Humanity on earth today. To the majority of souls in Utah, Jesus was known as a condemning God in the far heavens, rather than a God of love and charity. Those few souls who understood our Jesus seemed filled with fear in regard to freedom of worship. They did not enjoy the fruits of freedom and zeal which the Indian and Chinese people were privileged to have. I wondered about the conversion of the Mormon people but learned nothing. Rather, it seemed our Lord was concerned about the conversion of His own people from the hand of fear which killed holy zeal in the broader knowledge of His Real Person on earth.

Suddenly we were on the West Coast and there, as in Utah, few souls seemed to grasp the true form of love and worship of His Humanity within them and in the Blessed Sacrament. Our Lord asked Saint Aloysius, "Make well the sea." At this command, Saint Aloysius rode his glistening black horse into the great Pacific sea, and on his return he answered our Lord in these words, "It is blessed for one hundred years." Then our Lord asked Saint Aloysius to plant the third banner. As Saint Aloysius was standing it in the earth, I realized he was placing it in my yard near its center.

Our Lord dismounted from His horse and stood as it were before me and said, "Many people will come to the shrine. My own Mother will come here. Souls will be enlightened to My Humanity, and new faith will be enkindled in many souls."

I seemed to fall to my knees in fear and thanksgiving and there, in a rapture of love, on the ground of earth as if for my Christmas gift, I noticed our Lord's magnificent sandal. It was breathtaking in beauty. Human words are as nothing in trying to describe its excellence. Somehow, it looked as though our Jesus had stepped into a bed of perfect seed pearls, which had clung to His foot in perfect rows thus forming a perfect sandal with straps, ties, and soles. As I kissed His sacred foot, I noticed from each pearl arose music and human tones in song, telling all about the Nativity. The words were so clear it seemed I actually looked with Saint Joseph into the beautiful face of our Blessed Mother holding for the first time the gaze of her holy Infant Jesus.

As I stood up, I found myself in the divine embrace of love where neither words or worldly understanding could begin to breathe its wondrous mysteries in His way of love. Nothing matters with Jesus but love and kindness.

A few minutes later, our Jesus informed me He Himself would foster the world's last devotion, the Mystical Humanity within souls. He told me I would be persecuted for His devotion but to remember always He could do all things, even to forgiving the greatest sins, and to remember that sometimes He has allowed the greatest sinners made new to open the greatest doors to Him. Jesus then looked to the holy angel and told him to dismount from the horse, leave the court of God's personal angels for the rest of finite time, and heed the prayers from souls who lived and fostered the Mystical Humanity devotion. Jesus prayed the first prayer that He would wish us to use to ask the care and protection from His angel in these words, "Oh, Angel from God's personal court of angels, guide and protect me, for Jesus is within me in the Little White Host."

As the great angel heard the sublime words of prayer from Jesus, he bowed his head in the greatest of devotion, handed Jesus his silver gloves, and walked away into the darkness of earth. Beautiful thunder from Heaven filled the earth with tidings of joy as the angel left the light of his Creator. While the rumblings were offering praise, our Jesus spoke to me these words, "Tell Dad Hession,[8] your good husband, and My prince, that they equally share in the joys of your grace: 'confirmed in grace.' I personally bless all your friends who have taken Me as their living companion within them hour by hour. My gift to them is My personal angel."

I knelt in thanksgiving for such a gift for my friends, and all I could say was, "I'm such a sinner. I'm such a sinner." Jesus answered me as I rose to my feet, "Yes, you are a little sinner, but your trust has made you whole again." As Jesus spoke thus, the question arose in my mind as to whom He referred to as His prince, for often He Himself is called Prince. While my mind was questioning His meaning the thought came to me, He meant Father Frank; as I thought about Father Frank, our Lord bowed His Head, smiled beautifully, and again said, "My prince."

Then I asked Jesus, "If they—Father Frank, Mack, and Dad Hession—commit mortal sin, let me suffer for them," and Jesus answered, "They won't." I understood they were confirmed in grace in its highest step outside of personal revelation from Christ Himself to them. I was then reminded by Jesus to write and write. He especially reminded me about the degrees of joy in Heaven for those in His church as well as for souls outside the fold.

Jesus continued, "When I imprint an image or scene on a rose petal, it is a sign that a soul, through My Humanity, has been as close to My Heart as you have been in My sash, even though they have no recollection of it."

8　Mr. John Hession, a family friend

As the light of the vision was dimming, I looked for the bracelet, which had at one time chained my former spiritual guide and myself to the Master's wrist, but it was gone, and Jesus spoke as He patted my shoulder, "Detachment, Cora, is the best. Just pray for him."

Christmas 1946

CHRIST'S SANDAL

Down from Heaven's glorious canopy of art, rose petals and sweet odors fell near my heart. And there, enshrined on sandy shores, stood the Master of all art. I knelt to kiss the Master's footsteps emblazoned on earthly shores, and then I saw His sandal—unexcelled in beauty—not for human hands to handle.

A thousand pearls from gray to gold, all in even rows, formed His sandal, making it resemble a golden rose on earthly shores. As I knelt to kiss the holy ground, I listened to each pearl herald in symphonic tones the story of Christ's Nativity.

"Oh hidden mystery in each pearl," my soul cried, "I see the cave all dark and cold, and Joseph with tear-filled eyes shielding in his arms our Blessed Mother and her unborn Son." Another pearl told its story of fervent prayer, and there on bended knee knelt Joseph with Mary in his protective arm. In an ecstasy of love and joy beyond the cares of earth, I watched with Joseph and Mary how the angels built a crib of lace and gold, and how the angel wings stood tall to form lofty tapers round the holy crib. And with them I watched and listened to a million angel voices in words of praise and love to God in the calm silence of earth's most holy night.

In the silence of the snowflakes falling and chill of night made warm and bright by angels' presence, Saint Joseph prayed in joyous praise as angels lifted from Mary's heart into his earthly arms his little newborn Jesus. Angels by the millions touched with tender fingers God's exquisite infant toes—ten little, pink rosebuds born to crush our foes.

As the vision ended and the golden sandal dimmed in vision's sight, I saw rose petals falling as if from my heart upon His sandal on the shores of time, covering one by one the Master's pearls and His life, and then the glorious canopy of art was gone.

January 18, 1947, Feast of Saint Peter's Chair
MYSTICAL HUMANITY FOUNDATION
Heart of Vigil Lights—His Friends

Hidden within the depths of myself, I placed myself in imaginary vision before Jesus in His tabernacle home. There in God's beautiful immersion for souls who love Him above everything else on earth, He gave me the grace of hidden pain, a pain of inconsolable sorrow, the knowledge of our captive state (souls' restrictions within the confines of the clay body). My soul sighed heavily in its agony these sentiments, "Limitations, oh limitations, there is nothing to satisfy thee. Thou are bound, as a captured prisoner in a mask of clay! Oh, hand of death, thou art kind in thy gift of freedom when thou dost break the potters' clay, there to release the eternal realities to the vision of the soul. Oh, soul of limitations, thou art little, yet in thy love for God in the finite world may feel released for a moment, but oh the sadness, oh the heartbreak of loss, oh the terrible chains of captivity are still great when on thy returning thou must care for the clay of weight, with its penalty of limitations in its loss of passability.[9] Oh, Beloved Jesus of my heart, lest I die of loneliness, let me feel Thy caressing love upon this clay form of mine, for even though I love Thee, I am limited in the love and care I would give to Thee, my God."

In the realities of the soul beyond the powers of the earth, I heard the gentle rustle of our Lord's robes of heavy silk. Suddenly it seemed as though I were kneeling before a communion rail in a foreign church not to the liking of my earthly memory. Jesus seemed to be tiptoeing toward me. His gestures, smile, and calm footsteps gave homage to the quietness and solemnity of His church. In front of me where I knelt and directly behind the communion rail stood a large, heart-shaped candelabra, filled with unlighted votive cups in the cheerful colors of blue, gold, green, and red.

Jesus smiled at me as He held up a long taper with which to light one by one the vigil lights in the candelabra. As He set aflame each

---

9   In another manuscript, titled "Creation—Adam and Eve," Cora uses the word *passability* to describe the gift of freedom (like that of angels) given to Adam and Eve prior to the fall. Because that gift was lost, we are subject to the earthly effects of Original Sin.

candle, He gave it a name—names of my closest friends—and then He knelt beside me, and we watched with the awe of reverence the little tongues of fire. They flickered as though speaking in a symbolic language about a desire of unwavering love for Jesus. Then, through the grace of God, I realized I was listening and watching the combined love of souls for a common purpose, a solemnization of authority and power for God and His desire through the union of souls as one for Him.

Jesus rose to His feet and spoke these words as He seemed to gaze in raptures upon the symbol of souls, "May the sublime calling of the Eternal Father bless each soul here represented with the grace of eternal love. Through them may His eternal love be manifest in and through each of their actions, words, and deeds. May their cloak of wisdom be a constant guide to a living motto, 'All for God's glory.' May each word, action, and deed remind them of humility, kindness, and charity, as if the whole world depended upon their actions in the moment, lest perhaps the earth dissolve into nothingness because of their fault through unfaithfulness to God. May their love and devotion to My Humanity be the fires and pillars of strength in the foundation to the world's last devotion, in the world's last half hour, My Mystical Humanity."

Jesus walked around the end of the Communion rail and stood facing the burning candelabra. There He seemed to embrace the burning heart of love and, as He walked backwards toward His tabernacle home, He carried the heart of love with Him. There in the great distance, the flaming heart grew smaller until it reminded me of an emblem of His love pinned over His Sacred Heart.

Before the holy vision dimmed before my soul's eyes, I was permitted to see each light burning brightly in the tiniest vigil lights over His heart, and Jesus spoke with the greatest of love and devotion these words, "The holy oil will never diminish as long as thoughts of love feed the tiny tongues of fires. Each flickering tongue is the symbol of tongues speaking of love of Me or neighbor."

During my vigil with Jesus on February 7, 1947, our Blessed Lord appeared to me as He had left me on January 18. He was wearing the tiny heart of vigil lights. They were beautiful in their holy light, more beautiful than before. Through an embrace of love, Jesus permitted me to gather bits of knowledge as fragments of love for my friends on earth, and the fragments told me how on January 18 when our Lord appeared before the holy courts of Heaven wearing earth's holy emblem, earth's fires of love, all the angels and saints had received great pleasure. Their rejoicing was majestic in its grandeur of understanding, for the lighted fires of His heart taught them one thing: the beginning of earth's last devotion, Christ's humanity among men, in the earth's last half hour of time. The pillar of strength had been accepted and loved by the Eternal Father, and now that desire of all saints and angels was about to materialize. Earthly time was now in its last half hour of existence and then sin would be no more, and potters' clay would hold no more the hidden life of limitations.

LONELINESS IN INEXPRESSIBLE DARKNESS

"Oh, inexpressible darkness, thou are incomprehensible in thy depths of loneliness when Jesus has gone away for a little while. Little by little, thou art even transported into my memory, and consciousness is saddened because thou, oh loneliness, hast cooled the flame of love in my soul through longing, waiting, and watching for Him.

"Yet I know, oh inexpressible darkness, thou are deliciously sweet and kind if I would but cease my foolish struggling and whisper quietly, 'Jesus, I know Thou are here, for even in darkness Thou art present.'

"Oh embraceable love, for just a moment draw me to Thy affections and reestablish my former love, better to follow Thee as one entranced, not knowing darkness from light, nor light from darkness, but as an infant of complete dependability, not knowing nor caring wither I go."

From out of radiant darkness, my beloved Jesus drew near to my soul. From the abyss of ravishing light in an elegance of a hundred exquisite lights, as if each color were a glowing furnace afire, there glowed alone in the darkness the Jesuit necklace of perfect diamonds.

My soul cried aloud, "I know He is here for He wears them. I know He is here for He loves them. I know He is here for He is always with them. Oh, Jesus, Thou art here, yet I am blind to the splendors Thou would show me. I am like thorny thistles caught on Thy golden slippers. Oh, Jesus, teach me through the Jesuit furnace of love to love the sweet fragrance of night, to love the hidden melodies of Thy heart in the night of a soul, for Thou art there in light and in darkness, desolation and bliss. They are all alike to Thee for Thou art everywhere, my God."

Then to my soul I cried, "Oh, soul, why art thou sad? Dost thou not know through love and obedience in the diamond furnaces on earth He is there, hidden in each furnace of bliss on earth?"

ANOTHER CHRIST

Our Priest

Christ's ambassador, our priest, made his sick-call visit to a friend. He blessed her and then sat down for a friendly visit. Her words of thanksgiving (the words symbol of all mankind, in praise and appreciation for a priest's kindness and visit of consolation) raised her thoughts to the love of God. While she was thus speaking her words of thanksgiving, her eyes glanced upon his priestly hands, those precious hands anointed for God, as they lay folded in his lap.

In God's beautiful way through grace, as souls pray for the safety of His consecrated sons, she quickly found her way into the realm of a soul's death—into a world of burning, ardent love through meditation, where even memory fails to the delights of earth. For well she knew the meaning and power of those anointed hands and, in God's embrace of love, she wanted to pray for the preservation and safety of all God's anointed hands.

She spoke slowly and quietly in a rapture of love to the father beside her, "Father, I love to look at your hands. They are so blessed. They are living ciboriums. They held the Creator this morning. I am not worthy of this sublime privilege, to gaze upon the visible hands of another Christ." Her eyes searched for the darkness of solitude, better to hide away from such a wondrous sight, and there, her spiritual eyes fell upon the scene of a thousand angels watching and venerating the august hands of the priest beside her. The song of veneration seemed to reverberate through her soul in this meaning, "Oh unmeasured love, oh unmeasured and incomprehensible bliss, we never weary with the sublime gift of admiration and love as we stand in awe before the shrine of anointed hands, the visible, living hands of another Christ on earth."

An angel spoke to the woman these words, "How blessed you are, oh mortal soul. You have not only looked upon those anointed hands but you have even dared to touch them when he greeted you. Do you know how blessed you are? Do you realize, oh body of clay, that you have touched Christ's divine nature through His holy grace of transfiguration in His other Christs, the priests on earth? If we could envy you, this would be the reason. You have touched God's divine nature when you touch those anointed hands. When you touch them, we stand aghast and wonder how you feel when your hand breaks through the golden light which transcends those anointed hands. Do you feel in your flesh the experience of power and its vast, unutterable wisdom proceeding from the Divinity hidden in those anointed hands? Yes, we wonder how you dare to touch them and, when we see those hands open Heaven's fountains of grace upon creatures and ourselves, we bow in adoration. All Heaven trembles when those hands open Heaven through the holy Name of God. Oh, mortal soul, govern thyself in the paths of perfection, better to reverence and give glory to those anointed hands, the living ciboriums now before you."

In fear and trembling through such demonstrations of grace, she glanced again upon those hands still folded as though in prayer and, in breathtaking knowledge, she saw the glowing hands of Christ in and through those anointed hands. They glowed with an inconceivable golden radiance. The Eternal Father was there, for always His divine essence in the grace of transfiguration shows eternal glory through those hands, and His brightness always glows according to the transfigured priest, as inch by inch he grows away from self and world.

The angel spoke again into her soul, "A priest's hands are not for his own sake, but rather should be in perfect union with God at all times, better to live continually with God, or until the illuminating image of God transcends the priest's complete being into the one true Christ. This is Christ's joy on earth, to relive His Resurrection in souls in complete transfiguration with and through His other Christs, His priests—not for the moment at Holy Mass when God speaks the holy words, nor for the hour, but for all time."

With the grace of eternal sweetness flooding her soul, the woman spoke to the priest, "Father, thank you for the care and devotion you give your hands of supernatural powers. In reality they are my hands as well as yours, for without them I could not expect Heaven's gates to open, nor would the grace of holy absolution to fall up on me, nor would death to be easy. Oh keep them as they are, golden in grace and pure in charity, not only for yourself, but for the whole world. They are the hands of exceptional grace and power. They are the hands of power to reach from earth into Heaven's ways for our salvation. Do you realize, Father, your hands have lifted me from certain eternal death in Hell when my faith waned and I walked slowly upon the brink of eternal blackness because of despair and mistrust? Then, Father, through God's own way of gentleness through you, you beckoned me from that awful darkness. You taught me the ways of trust through my believing that you were God's ambassador, another Christ, and that I must follow you as I would follow Christ Himself. Your courageous hand in blessing, Father, was like another uplifted cross on Calvary pleading for my soul to listen and believe. I could not look into your eyes and not believe you were the Way, the Truth and another Christ. I then resolved to follow you into the paths of God's eternal glory because you are His image through your love of daily denials, mortifications, and penances against all inordinate affections to the world. Oh, Father of transfiguration, your golden hands—as though sheathed in golden gauntlets in His power of golden love—are unspeakably beautiful in the beauty of His powerful radiance. Father, through that radiance in your way of blessing and forgiving, you offer us your gems of glory and power, gems to become His reflected love through transfiguration. Oh most august and holy anointed hands, make me worthy of you, your trust and care. Humble this wayward soul of mine into the likeness of our God's childhood, where with childlike eyes I may better follow you and your uplifted hand of love and correction as you govern my way of life and show me the ways of trust. I must and will follow you as I would follow Him. Father, you rebuilt my lost faith, and now all that I receive from God is yours. You enkindled hope when courage died and led me to the light of everlasting grace through you. Then I saw, in you, God's way to human hearts. You were kindness and all-forgiving. You were calmness with gentle firmness. You were patience with dauntless courage to help win the fight for losing souls. You were meekness because you practice the virtues of prayer in the hidden knowledge of His transfiguration in you. Your gentleness makes you a master. You are a master of souls through God because of those anointed hands and His ever-growing transfiguration in you. How good God is. He is the gentle pursuer, following faithfully and patiently to gain your entire soul. Your smile is Christ's reflection, which tells of hidden eternal joys awaiting us who follow His other Christ into the higher paths to God—all this, Father, for us, through your anointed hands."

As the woman's voice ebbed into the silence of holy tranquility in the love of God, she was allowed to watch, through holy vision's grace, into the light of an early dawn where the Father who was visiting her stood vested and ready to offer the Holy Mass. His head was bowed as he walked quietly and slowly to the altar of sacrifice. From his heart, as though timed with the sweet chords of Heaven's music, there arose to the Eternal Father prayers of reparation, praise, and adoration as he neared the sacred altar. Then from far above in Heaven's fairways, there showered toward earth a beam of light which flooded over the altar like a golden waterfall. At such a wondrous sight, the woman's soul sang these words of delight, "Oh heavenly light from somewhere, you wing Yourself toward earth each day to lighten and gladden the path all other Christs must tread. Oh beautiful light from somewhere, come into this kind father's heart and, in vision's sweet love, give him the grace of pure prayer, better for him to love You, Eternal Father, as he ascends into the Holy of Holies, the unknown cloud of gold which is as real today as in the ages past when It glowed in desert paths before the chosen people."

As the vision of the Mass died away, the woman spoke again to the father beside her, "Father, when you are before the holy altar, do you realize you are our intellect, our desires, our hope, our trust, for only you can enter into the cloud of the Holy of Holies to plead our need, ask forgiveness for our sins, and offer God adoration as we never could if we spent our entire lives in adoration's prayer? As another Christ, you are allowed to unite the eternal heavens with the finite earth and all it contains through your entrance into His divine Countenance in the golden cloud of the unknown. Reposing in your hands as you walk up the altar steps to the painless Calvary is a tiny piece of bread, the symbol of all earth and all it contains. Your anointed hands, Father, place that piece of bread into the flaming heart of the Divinity which now surrounds you and the altar like a mantle of golden mist. And, in that sublime moment, Jesus Himself possesses you, and through you He speaks in His grace of transfiguration, 'This is My Body.' Your trembling, anointed hands now hold the sublime gift, the Bread of Heaven, to both earth and Heaven, for it has been in Heaven through your hands. Through your hands and Jesus possessing you and speaking, 'This is My Body,' Jesus dissolved that earthly piece of bread in God, and all that is dissolved in God, is God."

The vision reappeared and the woman spoke again, "Oh anointed hands in God's holy light, your charity for us is kind and courageous. Holy priest in God, as you bow in humble thanksgiving in the light of God, you kindly remember us who kneel in awe and astonishment before the Divinity and your sublime power and courage to step into the unknown for us. There in vision's knowledge, we hear your thoughts ringing throughout the world of sound, 'I must take Thee, oh my God, to your little ones who await Thee and Thy love outside the veil of Thy Divinity.' Then into the holy chalice, you breathe the breath of life as Jesus again speaks through you these holy words, 'This is My Blood, Eternal Father, which I offer to Thee for the remission of the sins of the world.'

"Then, Father, you slowly turn toward us with the remembrance of your promise to bring God to us. There in your anointed hands, for your adoration, flicker the little tongues of fire in the ciborium. Our God, our Creator, comes to us through your hands in this humble way in a piece of Bread made God, better for us to become enveloped in His lucent reflections and affections while we yet live on earth."

As the woman received the Sacred Bread made God in meditation's world of prayer, she cried aloud, "Oh hands of unknown power, oh hands of love and blessings, you are the hands of God, for those hands have led the way for us who receive the Sacred Bread in its humble form into the exquisite abyss of love, in the light from somewhere as It wings Itself to earth each day to illuminate your path with the light of the Trinity."

The woman's eyes gazed tenderly upon the priest's hands as they still lay folded in his lap, and she said aloud, "Oh immortal, anointed hands in God's exquisite reflections and devotion to us, bless me and heal my sinful soul. Make me like unto the flaming image of God through the grace of transubstantiation, for your hands can do this, Father. You can break me into nothingness, and in nothingness, like the symbol of bread, you may take me into the light of the unknown because you are another Christ on earth."

While yet in meditation's rapture, the woman asked God to bless the priest before her and, as the priest bowed his head to join his prayers with hers, there before her knelt not the priest, but Christ Himself. To the woman, Jesus spoke these words, "This priest's glory within Me is beyond explanation. His nature in Me cannot be comprehended for, inch by inch, he has found his way with Me, through me, and in Me. His complete emulation of [My] will and self brings Me the pleasure of constant transfiguration in him. I am allowed this pleasure in only one out of a thousand of My priests. I bless you through him, for him, and by him, for he is your will, the government of your soul, and the key to My eternal kingdom for you."

GOLDEN DETACHMENT IN THE SOUL

As the last words of "Our Lord's Forty Days in the Desert," were written, I knelt in prayer to thank Jesus for His gift of knowledge and for the gift of writing He had given me. This gift He had given me better to express His life and infinite love in our world of finite word expressions, through the gift of the contemplative life where human words seem ugly and unrefined and appear to a soul in love with God like clumsy brushes in the hands of an artist.

As I continued to pray, I suddenly felt the wondrous nearness of Jesus Himself, and there He stood before me in all the splendor of His divine Humanity. My soul before Him, like a poor weak prisoner, felt the suffering of my nothingness and slowly, as if under His silent command, I gazed into His eyes. His returning, understanding gaze of love gave me courage to remain kneeling in adoration before His real, unspeakable majesty. His voice, like a ravishing, abandoning delight to all the senses, pierced my soul with these words, "Cora, do you realize the gifts you have and could you love Me more if I gave you more?"

My soul seemed to wither at the thought of such questions, and I tried to reason within myself for an answer in the relation of wisdom to God. While I thus remained in silent thought, I was transported in spirit into a moment of God's eternal light. There, sudden illuminations of knowledge bathed my soul in the deeper gifts of divine understanding, and there I answered Jesus in wordless freedom of soul in the delights of His radiant silence. I do not remember how I answered Jesus, but I remember how, in one second, it seemed I traveled through the silent, mysterious past two thousand years. In those terrible and profound depths and in the hidden love of each gift of knowledge, I felt God's invisible, enkindling wisdom, judgments, and love fall across my soul like the shadow of a cross, there to burn with His light the ever-knowing judgment on myself. I was most unworthy of such delights and gifts. I was but a poor, weak creature filled with suffering emotions because I had not walked the narrow path of perfection with the higher grace of perfect resignation to my own will in little things. With the knowledge of such tremendous gifts flooding my soul and the knowledge of my unworthiness from the light of God, I remember I could not answer the second part of His question, "Could I love Him more if He gave me more?" For well I knew the contemplative gaze upon Jesus and His powerful glory in the essence of God. To gaze into His eyes with an answer in earthly words of praise or explanation would be a hindrance for the soul's expression, but silence with a look of love spoke the golden musings of wisdom in all answers for the soul, as earthly eyes saw in vision before them the glory of Jesus.

In those moments of delightful musing, just looking into His holy eyes, I longed above everything else to remain childlike to Jesus and not have my love for Him measured by supernatural gifts. Then memory reminded me my will was not my own. I had offered it to God. I had no right to make such decisions in the fields of grace. Father Frank was the lawmaker of my soul in the gifts of the spiritual life. I must consult with him about the question, "Could I love Jesus more if He gave me more?"

Again our Lord's ravishing voice asked me, "Cora, do you realize the gift you have? This is the first time I have given to the world such details of My life. I am giving this gift through you, better to establish My Kingdom of love within souls. I desire all souls to know I am real, alive, and the same today as after My Resurrection. For My kingdom in souls to be better known is another step in the golden age, golden because souls in sanctifying grace resemble the light of the golden, noonday sun. In that golden kingdom, I may personally dwell if I am invited, for I have said, "The kingdom of God is within you." Through this knowledge many souls still loan Me their bodies. Thus they actually become My Mystical Humanity, and in them I relive My life on earth as I did after My Resurrection."

I could not answer nor thank Jesus for His great gifts. All thoughts of gratitude seemed to freeze upon my lips. I knelt to kiss the floor where He stood, and my soul cried out these words to Him, "Oh crucible love, keep me ever near Thy Heart. Oh crucible love, give me the memory of Thy voice. May it be to me my life, my death, and my resurrection."

From the fold in His gown near His heart, Jesus removed a large golden lock, its half-circle arm or hasp closed into the main part of the lock. I noticed the lock was without a key. Jesus graciously handed me the lock and, as He did so, He spoke these words, "Here, Cora, ask Father Frank."

The vision ended, and, as I recollected myself, I could not understand what I should ask Father Frank. However, I resolved to tell him the complete story and follow his advice.

Later in the day I related the story to Father Frank. After much thought, he advised me to allow God to have His way in my soul and to accept any gift our Master desired for me to have, trusting Jesus would protect me against foolish pride, and to offer all the gifts and especially the one of writing as an act of continuous praise for the glory of God. And also to remember, after having asked my spiritual director for guidance and permission to receive God's graces, I would be doubly protected from the attacks of the devil in his quest to discourage my soul in the love of God.

Father Frank asked me to write the knowledge of the vision and the words of Jesus to me. I felt useless in the gift of writing and threw myself into the mercy of the Holy Spirit with this prayer from my heart, "Oh Holy Spirit, hold me in Thy light. Protect and govern me in understanding and will. Teach me the language of celestial essence for the earth, for I have seen many things without seeing and those gifts which I have seen were understood and loved in the soul alone and above earthly eyesight, yet I must write about them. Oh Holy Spirit, I know You understand how I long for solitude and quietness of inner thought. It is truly a world with expressions but without words. Oh Holy Spirit, guide my hand in writing for the continuous praise of God."

The next evening my soul was caught up into an ecstasy of love with Jesus in the same manner and expression of love as I had experienced in 1945, and again I felt myself as a tiny infant in the holy arms of Jesus as He skated over the ice of my heart, the symbol of growing detachment from the things of the world. The ice was not gray and cold-looking as in 1945 but glowed in a golden cast of rising mists.

Instantly I was no longer an infant but a grown woman walking beside Jesus on the golden sea of warmth and color. Jesus spoke, "This, the ice of your heart, is no longer drab and cold. Through its first steps in detachment to the world, it has blossomed and grown in the steady light of sanctifying grace until it is no longer you but the light of My love in your reflecting as a star between Heaven and earth for the good of souls." As we walked on, there before us lay a narrow, golden path, circling out from the main sea of golden ice into the eternal silence and pleasing darkness to the soul of detachment. Then I understood the narrow path was the hasp of the golden lock which Jesus had handed me the day before, when He asked directed me to ask Father Frank. The golden lock was the symbol of my heart.

As we began to walk on the narrow pathway, Jesus spoke, "We are walking upon the lock, the symbol of your heart. Your soul is one lock of many locks to My heart. The knowledge which you have received has been your unlocking My heart through perfect trust that I would give you anything for the use of My glory. From this minute on, you hold the key to My heart. In the wisdom of trust, you may unlock My treasures at will through the governing powers of Father Frank. Other souls may become keys to this way of love by walking upon the narrow path of perfection on which we now are, after they have turned a deaf ear to the callings of the world and its forbidden pleasures—forbidden if they forget Me as their constant companion. Detachment must be put to a test, not for a day nor a week, but for several years. This way of perfection may be gained for all vocations in life. The fruits of the narrow path are simple, childlike prayer, just talking to Me in My Humanity through the gates of the Blessed Sacrament. Incredible calmness is next, calmness to the extent that life becomes a joyous thought of willingness to please Me above everything else, both in sorrows and joys. Self-immolation is next. Do for others before considering thine own self, even in little pleasures of the world. Deny thyself that others might have. This purification on earth corresponds to a state of Purgatory which is known on earth as the state of holy souls. There they, too, commune with angels of consolation and talk to fellow men who are also in Purgatory. There they learn detachment as if they were given another chance on earth. However, these souls learn and practice detachment in another sense, for they are spiritual; nevertheless, both worlds of detachment are equally hard to master." As we neared the center of the circling hasp of the lock, or the narrow path of gold, we stopped to look into the dark depths of eternal nothingness, resembling a dark sea which lay between the main lock and the circling hasp. Jesus asked, "Do you see anything in this mirrored darkness?" I answered, "No."

Jesus continued, "If you should be so unfortunate as to leave this narrow path, I may have to bring you here from time to time to show you the attachment on earth which you have placed above the thought of Me. I assure you, to vision any love above the love of Me in this darkness would be most painful to both soul and body and equally comparable to the suffering in Purgatory."

I remember shuddering at His words, and silently I prayed for the grace never to fail my Jesus, for I feared above everything else to be walking alongside Jesus and have my sins mirrored before me rather than His kind smile of love. As we walked on toward the main part of the lock, Jesus spoke to me in a most beautiful and humorous way, "This is a very narrow path, Cora. It is only wide enough for two, just you and Me. When you could not answer Me as to whether you could love Me more if I gave you more, it was because your soul ever feels the gift of obedience though your soul's advisor, Father Frank." Then with a smile He continued, "I could almost become jealous over your solicitude and obedience to Father Frank above Me, but he is another Christ, and that is the way of obedience, all through the will of My priests. Souls are privileged to follow this way of obedience, for only through My priests' guidance can souls walk upon the gold their own hearts in its way of purgation. While they live on earth, there is no other way to the higher way of perfection."

As we walked on in silence, I realized I must walk alone down into the depths of the lock. I understood my body and soul represented the secret key. It would unlock the lock, thus releasing the hasp, and I wondered if this would be the moment of my death to earth. Would this be the living death which Saint Paul spoke about in writing, "I die daily," or would this be a living death from time to time, better for me to lift from His hidden treasures the knowledge and hidden meanings in Christ's life on earth? These questions raced through my mind as I descended into the lock and, as I took each step, I felt the radiance of unequaled grandeur of light revolving about me and coming from inside the lock. Light, like revolving rainbow arches, one after another, as far as the spiritual eye could see, rolled toward and over me. There in those arches of unexplainable inexplicable glory stood thousands of angels, all in human form, adoring God in an act of deepest reverence to the thought of God. As I stood watching, I seemed to fall into a rapture of dreadful pain, pain to both body and soul, a type of pain which I had never experienced. Yet it was most beautiful and pleasing to the soul as well as terrifying in excessive exhaustion to the human body. I did not plead for mercy, for I seemed to understand it was a pain of purgation, necessary to have to be near the angels of great holiness. Suddenly all the angels turned toward me. From their eyes there seemed to flow great, narrow streams of living fire all directed at my heart. As each flame left its burning delight upon my heart, I felt the joy of desiring to love Jesus more and more.

As the vision ended and I left the vastness of the interior lock, I heard my soul addressing the Holy Spirit in these words, "Oh, Holy Spirit, don't ever leave me. Take me by the hand and lead me on the narrow path. There instill in all my senses the knowledge that I must love God more and more. Never, never, oh Holy Spirit, let me fall. Never let me see the world's gifts in the sea of blackness in the place of our Christ's Holy Face."

January 31, 1948

VICTIM SOULS (I)

In the world of interior freedom, in the ecstasy of God's embrace of love where the desire to love Jesus sways the complete will into a state of loving Jesus above all earthly desires, it was there I pleaded with God to guide me in His way of wisdom and enlightenment on the hidden depths of victim souls, for I had been asked by Father Frank to write the knowledge which had been given me in a timeless second while I was in ecstasy on January 4, 1948.

Suddenly my soul felt the freedom of indescribable sweetness. Jesus in all His glory was near me, yet I could not see Him. But through His wonderful way of spiritual gifts to a soul, I found myself looking into the breadth of endless space—a space without sound, a space filled with intimate meaning in the wisdom and knowledge of victim souls. From blue depths of nothingness, there arose thousands of great, crystal-clear pinnacles, all dazzling in their purity of color like a shimmering frost on church steeples. Some pinnacles were towering in height to become awesome to the spiritual sight, while others were of less height but equally beautiful. I noticed the majority of the pinnacles were of one standard height, while a few others here and there seemed endless to the intellect of the soul. I learned through God's wisdom in my soul that these pinnacles were the symbols of victim souls to God's love, all in different vocations of life.

Then my invisible Jesus spoke, "These very tall pinnacles are the many captains in My army. You will notice one pinnacle is not dependent upon another. Their light, their love, and eternal height are for Me alone. It is through them, who reach the deepest into My Heart, I pour upon earth my gifts and graces for souls and nations. They are too lofty in their love of solitude and detachment to wonder about My plans and to whom I give the meritorious graces they have earned through the steps of perfection in the way of love. These captains are so tall they look strong, but they are the most fragile, for if they weaken through fear, they have the greatest fall. Because they are alone in solitude to the world, they feel the worst of storms, yet they are the first to receive the morning sunlight of graces, for they have weathered the storms of earthly and spiritual evil and, with their mighty protecting strength through solitude and calmness, they have shielded many weaker souls as they slowly climb My way of love."

As the beautiful voice of Jesus died away, there before me stood our Jesus in the glory of His Humanity dressed as a bishop and carrying a crosier covered with rubies and diamonds. As I knelt at His feet, He quoted these words, "Many are called but few are chosen." As Jesus spoke those solemn words, there before us rose the great valley of pinnacles. Jesus continued, "Into great classifications I have placed the honored, 'chosen' few. The chosen few are the real captains in My army. They are the victim souls to My love. They are victims because they are seasoned through study and prayer in the knowledge of the all-sufficient God—God sufficient without them and not needing any help they may offer Him. Thus, in great humility of soul, their torch of light in souls' darkness is the light of trust in the providence of God above their own will. True captains know the steps of discipline because they have guarded well the spiritual fire entrusted to their souls. Victim souls to God's love, symbolized by the tallest pinnacles, are such because they recognize they are nothing and stand before Him clothed only in His merciful robe of trust. Thus they stand like children, lovingly gazing upon the beauty of God in everything, awaiting His least command in any of the virtues such as purity, gratitude, pain, sorrows, love, or any other virtue which they feel inclined to follow after much prayer and under the guidance of My priests. Victim souls have practiced detachment and well understand the merit of detachment. They well understand the love of holy indifference to petition and self-want. They trust in God's wisdom for He knows their every need and, through an act of love, thus forgetting self, they are granted all their desires because God cannot be outdone in generosity. They strive for the sublime sleep of the contemplative victim through the steps of meditation. They thrive on and love the knowledge given them through the earth-like martyrdom, better to become totally disengaged with their own desires. In the sleep of contemplative love, they relish the gift of God's spiritual communion as though it were constant and never-ending. In that embrace of love, they offer all passing desires and intentions to God in one pure act of love, like unto our priests offering the chalice in the Holy Sacrifice of the Mass filled with intentions, love, and adoration, thus believing through faith that Jesus Himself will offer to God all we lack and making imperfect prayers perfect. Those captains clothed only in the robe of trust sing aloud this song as they think of God in constant communion, 'Oh God of love, do with me as Thou will. I have given Thee my memory, my will, and understanding and now, clothed in trust, I stand as a flickering flame before Thy divine Mercy, without purpose or intention. Oh passable God of true love, come, and through me do with me as Thou will.' Souls thus believing and trusting in the first principle of trust without fear are the seraphs of earth. They are of the highest order in the communion of the saints on earth. They are the real heroes and doers on earth for both souls and nations. In the mind of God, they are like a beautiful necklace of diamonds to be worn or discarded as the great God wills for His pleasures. Without question or complaint, these captains are content just to wait, enthralled in patience and trust before the nearness of God's splendors, knowing through them the Master finds His pleasures."

February 1, 1948

VICTIM SOULS (II)

"Oh, sympathetic truths striking upon my heart from God's eternal embrace," my soul cried, "How can I imprint the finalistic principle of love into the error of earthly language?" Into the sweetness of hope, my soul arose in prayer to God the Holy Spirit for guidance in my infirmity in the knowledge of taking away from God's embrace of unspeakable language and in that which I take away in memory under obedience to Father Frank. "Help me to make application in word similitude to that which is still seraphic knowledge as it pounds like music within my soul."[10]

Then my memory recalled my guide and companion, Saint Aloysius, and I asked him to help me with the crucible pain of knowing an unspeakable knowledge which must be put into words for the glory of God. Into the penetration of my own soul, I felt the intimate nearness of Saint Aloysius. It seemed as though he sat beside me while I typed and listened to his way of simple explanation.

Saint Aloysius began, "A victim soul is a specialist in God's great Church. The mystical body of the Church needs more specialists to specialize in certain virtues. The ranks of victim souls are thinning

---

10 Editor's note: Cora prays for the ability to render into words that which transcends the power of language to express (i.e., angelic or seraphic knowledge).

as never before since the real time of Christ on earth. Victim souls specializing in any one of Christ's virtues are similar to souls who willingly make the heroic act. They give to God all the merit they may gain during the day, or periods of years, or for a lifetime, all to be applied to souls in Purgatory. Thus they are always in true spiritual poverty of soul, dressed in the gown of trust, believing God will not be outdone in generosity. Thus, in their poverty of soul and love or charity in being merciful to the souls in Purgatory, they gain great merit, greater merit in one second than if they were to read highly indulgenced prayers every moment of a natural life. The same principle can be applied to God's other victim souls, souls who wish to specialize in one other virtue but do so with greater spiritual poverty by not dictating to God what to do with the merit which they have or may gain. Rather they give all to Christ to do with as He wills without question, command, or wonderment. They too, like little children, just stand in the robe of perfect trust, trusting in joy in God' providence in all things."

I asked, "Saint Aloysius, tell me in this simple language what souls must do to gain the desire and grace to become victim souls or specialists in any one of Christ's fields of virtue."

Saint Aloysius answered, "First it is necessary for souls to become masters of themselves in the order of self-discipline in curbing the five senses, better to become a sensitive victim to the nearness of sin and then, in the laws of penance, to establish peace and calmness in order to live the higher life of solitude and self-denial in a spirit of joyfulness. Secondly, souls should study the lives of the saints and especially acquaint themselves with the knowledge of interior living with Christ, the true, intimate living with Christ as the saints have known. Thirdly, when a soul feels the desire to please God above everything on earth, it is wise to receive a confessor's consent to kneel silently before the Blessed Sacrament and offer one's self as a victim soul to his or her choosing in any one of Christ's virtues. It is a wise and holy custom to offer the morning offering, for it is prayer without ceasing as Saint Paul teaches. Therefore in offering oneself as a victim, a soul's every act and move that day earns merit, and God takes that merit and applies it where or how He wills for the good of souls or for nations. When souls ask for prayers, it is wise to remember them in this way,

'I love You, Jesus. Bless my friend,' for no petition is greater than to ask God's blessing on friends. Therefore, like tiny infants who cannot speak (spiritual childhood), we entrust petitions through an act of love. Be not overburdened with sets of prayers but rather, while working or playing in chosen vocations, remember to say a thousand times a day, 'I love you, Jesus,' thus recalling to mind the former offering of self as a victim of His love. The Mass prayers, the Office, the rosary, and Stations are all great merit-making gifts to be given to God to do with as He wills. If possible while in daily tasks, souls should desire to receive Jesus in the Blessed Sacrament in a spiritual communion a thousand times a day. Thus in this passable way of love in God, they become a living tabernacle, and through them Christ does all things for the love of God."

BRIDGE OF MEDITATION INTO HIS HEART

Rest and sleep in Him, oh soul of mine. Rest in holy rest in this thy hour of prayer with Jesus. Oh, soul, how sweet and sublime are the captivating wonders He joyously shows thee.

My soul cried, "Jesus, my beloved, all these gifts and holy wonders which Thou dost show me leave me fearful lest I forget them. For when they are breathed in the breath and tone of earthly words, Thy sublime gifts seem like mere fantasies. Yet I know in the world of meditation, fantasy in earthly terms is beauty. Therefore, through sensible reasoning, fantasy is real, for all good thoughts come from Thee. Reasoning in the world of meditation makes fantasy or beauty beyond imagination. They—beauty in Thy thoughts—become the steps in meditation's delights for souls better to climb in their quest for Thee in Thy Humanity.

"Souls thus in search of Thee, my Jesus, step quietly and surely upon the great bridge of meditation which leads from their hearts into Thy immensities. There, hidden in Thy immensities of knowledge, the body sighs as though dying because of beauty and its sublime understanding in Thee through Thy reflections on the body through the hidden soul. Souls thus engaged on the bridge of sighs walk on and on until they feel lost, as if they were nothing in Thy immensities. Yet soul breathes on because of enjoyment in Thy sublime gifts, oh my Jesus of wondrous charity."

There at once it seemed I stood upon an endless bridge, a bridge with its beginning in my heart, better to fashion for my delights an endless chain of steps leading, I knew, into the light of God. Each step reminded me of a closed book or a day in my earthly life. As I stepped upon one and then another, I heard whispered voices of praise and melodies telling me of virtues well practiced in the days gone by in my life. I walked on and on, step by step, listening to God's way of hidden delights and melodies, and from them I learned the greater need of prayer and courage to overcome selfish faults which sounded in my soul as hushed notes, telling me only of neglect. A few books or steps were silent, and well I remembered they were the days of neglecting my Jesus. They were silent days that told me of search for joys on earth above my Jesus. Other steps or books chimed like a thousand bells ringing in a joyous mood, and I understood they were the tones of angels' praise to God and which would last for all eternity in praise for my poor soul because it had tried to win a victory over sin.

My soul seemed to bend and weep over my sad neglect in past years, and in bitter sorrow I gazed heavenward, better to say, "Forgive me," and there, walking toward me on the bridge of sighs, was our wonderful Jesus.

Suddenly I watched my own soul reflected in its sinful, dimmed light upon the mirrored brightness of our Jesus in His sacred Humanity. His tender gaze and assurance of love in His embrace of understanding gave me courage to gaze upon my sinful self as if hidden in His light and I breathed aloud, "Oh, merciful Jesus, burn away my sins. Burn away my body. Burn away my soul and let me live in Thee. Content I'll never be until I am with Thee, through Thee, and in Thee. Oh, mirrored brightness, hide me in Thy light. Hide my sinful soul beneath thy feet, and there forever my delight will be complete."

My soul before His brightness dimmed into a mere shadow near His sacred Humanity, and I sensed these earthly thoughts as if He were allowing me to remember them as lessons for myself and friends. What do I say when near Him on the bridge of sighs? As if it were a living essence apart from my soul, my reason seemed to answer me in this manner, "With Jesus I need say nothing for He is everything, all powerful and filling every need, care, and mood, for He knows our least desires. Even understanding is a useless essence and unnecessary in the immersion of love with Jesus. For in that great dissolving, even for a moment whilst souls live yet on earth, understanding is like a bird released from a cage. Neither does it first hesitate to wonder to where it shall fly, but flies in joyous release into the exquisite freedom where beauty, music, and eternal truths mingle as one knowledge and where restrictions are never felt, never known."

My soul deeply hidden in His beautiful light asked, "Jesus, my beloved, if it is Thy will for souls better to understand true flight to Thee after they have tried to conquer self through sense mortification and obedience to Thee and to the laws of their chosen vocations in life, how may they find Thee in the greater heights of love on the bridge of sighs?"

Jesus answered, "It is I who call souls to the greater light of knowledge, either in real death or sleep of repose through meditation. I have promised to a few souls on earth a foretaste of Heaven. Upon those souls who have tried to make perfect their wills in Me through self-mortification and who have tasted the delights of knowledge through meditation upon My life and spoken word, I breathe My gifts as I venture upon the bridge which leads Me into their hearts. Thus in their hidden prayer of repose for Me, I am enthroned for a second, while in other souls I am enthroned for days and years. These souls I often beckon to leave their own hearts and come to meet Me upon the bridge of sighs made beautiful by detachment to the world for love of Me. The bridge of sighs is rightly named, for indeed the body sighs in its union with its God and, knowing it must leave the sanctuary of delight for its earthly mission, the soul weeps and the body sighs as though dying from a broken heart. Living death to these souls strikes hourly, and hourly they allow Me to resurrect in and through them, thus allowing Me to borrow their body as a mystical body for My delights, better to give the world My graces of love. These generous souls are My delight on earth.

"My first inner call is to souls thus entering upon the bridge of sighs in the world of higher meditation where they forget their own existence and thus in souls' repose fly into My arms. I permit them to feel the hidden warmth of My love (knowing I am near) and to sense deeper love. These graces thrive though love into a love above everything else on earth, a love wherein worded prayers seem useless. Petitions seem troublesome, and true trust in the one thought of perfect love encompasses all the desires of verbal prayers of praise, glory, thanksgiving, and petition. In the sleep of hidden repose, love *alone* understands love. Love thus in repose is the essence of God, for God is the highest and all love above everything else.

"When a soul thus tastes this holy love, I give them the sleep of souls' repose where for a moment or perhaps hours I find personal rest and comfort as you often experience in the calm, quiet rest in a church alone with Me as your silent Guest. Upon souls in the sleep of repose where only love is understood, I pour My greatest graces. They are My living fountains of grace to the world. A soul thus lost in the quiet of love does not completely withdraw from the earth in all its natural senses, for the essence of knowledge cannot be quieted even on the holy way of meditation. Essence of knowledge thus causes souls to realize they are with Me, either in an embrace of their nothingness or as a receiver of knowledge which cannot be erased from souls' minds that are thus entrusted with the divine mission of forming in earthly words a reality which does not touch the senses as do true earthly adventures. The embrace of nothingness of self or partial dissolve into God is complete nothingness for a moment; that moment cannot be understood nor remembered in the slightest degree after repose of sleep in God. The essence of knowledge, even in a dimmed degree before Me, causes souls to realize love and so, in the sleep of repose, mind is not a silent void but rather is love based on knowledge. Thus knowledge leads souls unmarred to the bridge where I meet all souls, either in real death or in the essence of sleep in death whilst they sojourn on earth."

I heard my soul repeating these words of prayer as I walked alone, retracing my steps over the bridge of love, "Oh wondrous God, enrich our lives with the knowledge of Thee in Thy Humanity. For through Thee our path to Thee is easy. Death is sweet because we know how to reach our souls to Thee through prayer. Thus we are never alone. Help us to remember Thy wish, 'My delights are to be with the children of men,' and help us to make our delights on earth Thy delight. I love Thee, Jesus."

PART TWO

Little Thoughts

Note: The publisher has organized the following statements by category and added headings to identify the subject matter. Cora referred to them as "Gems" or "Little Thoughts."

EUCHARIST

Communion is to receive Him in the Little White Host; it is to converse with Jesus alone. O sublimest of graces—Christ alone with me and I am permitted to speak!

O Little White Host, why do you flutter like a wounded dove in my heart? Is my soul cold and bare—like tall white cliffs in a storm—to Thy warming love? How I would like these tall cliffs to resemble warm sunshine of Thee. O little, fluttering White Host, let me fly away with Thee into God's holy light, there to be warmed and arrayed in His warmth of glory, better to return to earth and make this body of mine Thy tabernacle of warmth and love.

When you are nothing but dust, O body, I hope in some mysterious way you'll find a way to visit the Blessed Sacrament. Perhaps in the airways of time, a tiny speck of me will find its course over the melting ore, which the goldsmith forms into a chalice to hold the Sacred Blood—and in that chalice I may be permitted to adore. Or perhaps on a dusty windowsill with a thousand other souls in the cloak of dust, I'll be content to adore the Master in the Blessed Sacrament. Or perhaps this speck of me will light upon a sacred host where I may say in the essence of accidental truths of that which once did really speak,

"I love Thee, O Blessed Sacrament." But O dust of me, in the folly of wishful thinking, rather would I have you find your way into the tiny grain of wheat, which in time would be baked into the little round wafer and then in turn that little wafer, through God's priest, is changed into the Body of Jesus—there would I be forever content—one in one with Christ's Humanity.

Life is a parable—daily we must find the clue it offers us to live by. Life is a treasure hunt for all to play, yet many fail to see the treasure even though their clues are many. The treasure, they ask, what is it? Christians answer, "The Little White Host is uplifted in the cupped hands of another Christ, our priest."

HUMILITY

November 18, 1945—Jesus said to me, "On this day, I'm flooding thy soul with joy and peace such as thou hast never known. Ask Father Frank to help you preserve it; let nothing disturb it."

I only wish to be the brush in Christ's artists' hands—better to let Him portray His Love for souls in and through His humanity.

Come, Holy Spirit, and guide me through this earth's trials. Whisper Thy gift of courage to me when the father of darkness casts his shadow across my path. Oh, merciful God, give me grace to know the good from evil.

Humility is a steppingstone in the path to Home. In this sublime thought, O soul of mine, take courage and step a little firmer on the rocky path. And when thou dost stumble because of pride from friendly tongues in their way of praise to thee, just step a little firmer and humbly say, "Thank you; all for Thee, my Jesus."

Our Beloved said, "To succeed, little soul, is to always remain recollected in My love alone."

MEDITATION AND CONTEMPLATION

Limitations or dullness of thought is because we close the inner door of self through fear of ridicule. Thus we lock the soul away from its

God, Who is the giver of all good thoughts. Cease to limit the soul in its quest to think good thoughts. Cease to limit the soul who soars aloft in imaginative realms to search for God, for a free soul dost not know limitations nor dullness in meditation. A lively meditation is life in God!

Every garden in the night within its shadows so dark and clear should reveal to us our Lord in prayer. If we listen closely, we may hear the sobbing of a broken heart for us who live without a care.

ECSTASY

Heaven's mist fell across my forehead there to shatter and fall in tears upon my face. Jesus, You are near!

A thousand beads, like a thousand little prayers of love, for love flutters like rosebuds in golden urns with the fragrance of holiness before the Blessed Sacrament. While scattered prayers, like scattered leaves along the way to Him, form a path to ecstasy where meditation's depths prove love for Love is the only joy on earth.

In my Beloved's mercy, while I still remain in this insupportable weight of unthinkable ugliness of earthly clay, I hope hourly to hear Him in His transactions and hopes of conquering myself against myself for His greater glory.

O twilight, thou art like a homing dove; thou hast come to embrace my soul in thy mantle of love as I kneel to whisper to Jesus of love. O twilight, breathe thou for me tonight of love and in thy way of silent prayer, whisper into every shrub and tree and flower my sentiments of love to God. And on the wings of morning light, may the tones of my love rise like a homing dove to fly into the morning sun, there to be forever dissolved in love for Love!

EYES OF THE SOUL

Skepticism is a staggering fault in a soul. Through the eyes of the soul in meditation's sleep, skepticism resembles an earthquake with all its disaster on earth. Skepticism does not hurt one, but many.

Whilst in prayer I asked Jesus, "Is it possible to measure the living soul with the scale of finite mind?" Jesus answered, "Imaginative power is encased within the soul. Measure the heights of governed imagination in its travels into the immensities or into the tiniest grain of sand, and you will have measured the soul. The soul like unto God is nearly everywhere—God is everywhere."

TIME

Many times I have wondered about the question of time in eternity. My angel spoke these words: "Time does not live; time does not die, for time does not exist. In Heaven, time is now and forever the same thought in God. If time died as finite mind understands it, then memory too would die, and memory is part of the soul and the soul is indestructible in time and eternity, and so time lives on forever in the soul of man, either on earth or in Heaven."

Time as to the world is pathetically sad—but where there is not time, the senses may become tuned to the cherished knowledge of love that lies beyond the mystery of speech, which depends on time. Where time and speech do not breathe, we may understand our souls are His, and in Him we may hear His murmured love as He speaks for us these words, "Bless one another. Forgive one another. Love one another. In My Kingdom you are one reflected tone in love for My delights."

GUIDANCE

Kind letters are like rays of invisible sunshine piercing the darkness of the soul.

Friends are like the refreshing raindrops scattering over the world as if they were shot from the Master's bow of everlasting charity, kindness, calmness, and joy. Friends, friends, friends—Jesus had them all—He loved them all and tried to see the best in all; therefore, He was loved by all. Even those who feared Him had fear because they were motivated by the spirit of love and not hate. Hate is the true enemy; hate is definitely evil and has no part with God or friends.

EXHAUSTION

O merciful God, how can I really be sure I love You, and could my professed love be an illusion? Our Master spoke, "Dost thou not often exhaust thyself in prayer, better to know and love Me? Exhaustion through prayer is but the burning gaze of the Eternal Father upon thy body and soul. God's love is exhausting to the body, but it is strength to the soul and death to the world."

LIGHT

Our character is animalistic—it is built by slow degrees, hourly changing for the better or for worse. Watch the pendulum and catch the light and take back with you His light into the valley of darkness, then swing again into His light—Christ is the Light of the World.

TRUST

Belief and believe, O little words, how much alike you are, yet you are so far apart in mutual love as if you were human friends in a quarrelsome mood. O my friends, thou art in defeat in thy way to God unless thou dost bring belief and believe under the mutual title of simple trust.

TRUTH

Don't search for truth until you know the rules. The Ten Commandments of God's will are the paths of golden rules; they are the pillars of truth.

Scientific men say science is an art—everything on earth is an art. Even the earth, like a toy, we pull apart to see just what made it start. "Scientific importance on the trends of the times," says another, "it is the way to a happy life." While the academic scholar says, "Economic knowledge is the courage of the races and the dignity of labor is the right to share the dollar." All these, the world acclaims, are the result and excellence of education; it is also courage of conviction and love and good will to all men.

All these proofs, the scientific men say, are learned through the science of the ages, for it is an art in new knowledge in the penetration of mind. But alas, what fools we mortals be!

All these things Christ taught, but we fail and we sin. Then we refuse Him the credit for academic minds and scientific skill, for He created them to be little channels of grace for less fortunate souls, who await their gifts for a better life as if they were rivers of protection—rivers of solace and comfort, peace and love. Let it never be said of great minds when they face the Creator, the giver of all these gifts: "We created that—we discovered that, we are the cause of this, we are the monsters who retarded God's way for souls." Rather, let them sing aloud when each new discovery is made on earth: "Christ is excellence in the phase of knowledge, for when we discover a newborn truth, we are discovering a little more of Christ—Christ is knowledge for the human race."

PAIN AND SUFFERING

Let us give attentive ear to Christ, the true physician, better to learn how to bear with pain.[11] Pain is an extra gift that He gives to a few souls in His divine plan of redemption, through God in us, for our fellow men.

Pain and its haunting fears,
We do not know their worth.

Pain and its taunting fear,
Make us know their worth.

Pain and its taunting fears
Often make one know their worth.

---

11 Publisher's note: According to Ruth Spaulding, Cora's sister, this was an exercise of Saint Aloysius—to compose a poem using pain and fear.

Pain and its taunting fear
Make us like gold of great worth.

Pain is the flower of holy grace,
Fear is the frost that kills.

O pain, teach me how to pray in the race,
Lest my body weaken in the frost that kills.

O sweet sorrow of sighs from my heart,
arise in beauty to my God and like the tones of a violin
take me on thy wings to Jesus.

Like unto the ever-coaxing, breaking sea, let our voices rise and fall to greet the knowledge of pain, trial, and sorrow, for through conquering self to accept these gifts with joy, we become His child of grace and love.

My soul cried aloud in pain, "Help me, Father, on this road of pain. I must walk alone—my heart beats alone—I don't like to complain. My soul is going down into the shadows of gloom—going down, going down all alone and I'm afraid. Help me, Father, along this road of pain, no one walks here but those in pain. Over rocks, thorns, and briars, I find my way and now I stop and ask: is this God's game? No one claims pain as their own—it is a gift from Christ's Holy Name. Father, must I walk alone—I don't like to complain, for I'm filled with vanity and questions 'why'—so filled am I with these questions that I'm afraid to venture into God's kind, gentle game. Father, I'm not worthy to walk this path where none doth roam but those in pain. Help me, Father, on this lonely road of pain."

Wisdom is lessons well learned through the cross of suffering day by day.

Sorrow is detachment from something on earth which we love. Joy is detachment from earthly pleasures and sorrows, better for us to look above.

My angel said, "Try to say, 'Now lead me on, ever on and on, the cross is sweet.'"

Slow sorrow is purgation while on earth. Do you not know that you compare with those souls who claim to be abandoned souls?

My soul cried, "O Jesus, let me hear Thy voice of sympathy, for sorrows in my heart would fill a book." I heard Jesus say, "Look into the eyes of the passerby and there see a greater sorrow than thine—many names are not written in My book."

PEACE AND HAPPINESS

Happiness in the world has only one equal—that is holiness, and that is not for us to attain unless we see Jesus in His creations and learn appreciation—that is holiness.

Peace and fear cannot dwell together—one or the other will win—which do you choose?

I asked a friend, "Are you happy?" The friend's eyes turned to me, and there I read the answer: "Happy only vaguely—for I am selfish and self-absorbed rather than giving Christ my entire self to do with as He wills."

EVIL AND FEAR

O God help me, my soul cried, in this valley of tears, for on this report card of my own soul the devil leers. Help me to make Heaven cheer when I learn to adopt the words You hold dear, for they read, "God commands and wills for me to be joyous, good, and merciful in life."

O Lord, deliver me from the devil's verse which reads, "I demand you rebel and continue to be hateful and bad in your revengeful strife in life."

The devil's tools are sloth, fear, discord, turmoil, and strife. All these are actual thieves.

A day of tears is often because one fears.

A pagan's grief is sad, when in fear he thinks of his own pending death. It is despair against hope of living again.

Souls in the state of grace have nothing to fear from the world, death, or evil, but they should live from day to day in a harmony of love and devotion, thinking perhaps tonight they may die in Me (Jesus).

Holy souls clothed in the grace of wisdom do not fear the whip of justice, and they are not bothered with powers and principalities of evil, which cause souls to question God.

Souls governed in the graces of love and knowledge of My justice know that the powers of anti-Christ are in the world today, striking hourly with his weapon of fear into the hearts of men with foolish questions and prophesies, whereas the end of time no man will know nor will the angels. The end of the world is when individuals die— their body is their world.

HERESY

O boundless charity, stem the tide of my friends in heresy,[12] as they grope in a modern fog-like screen of broadmindedness. Littleness they think, when through love we live the Ten Commandments.

You can hear heresy. It is a beast preying on souls whom he may devour. Listen, he is as sounding brass, loud castanets, and desert tom-toms; they tell of his raging pacing for you and me.

It is wisdom to learn the folly of powerless gods, for one soon learns none can give internal peace to mind and soul.

MERCY

Jesus, I am lonely for Thee tonight; life no longer holds contentment, for Thou has shown me Thy Holy Face. No beauty or pleasure remains; even the gold of sunsets and the blue of the ocean depths still my heart with longing for Thee, for through the vision of Thy Holy Face, the world did melt away. O God, everything on earth is but a mere reflection of Thee—have mercy on the interior sight that longs for Thee.

Mercy is the unbridled mind of God. Compassionate mercy is God-Man running toward us with pierced feet to show us an easier way home. Mercy is to desire and pray, whilst compassion is to act and obey.

12   Publisher's note: Cora refers here to Mormonism.

Confession is a temporal and eternal gain, and if we fall again in sin and lose the game, the gems of grace—just plough through the soul of dust until you see the gems. Then hurry to thy confessor, the keeper of those gems, and let him whose hands are worthy pick up the gems and dust the dust away for the love of Him our Eternal King.

God gave the world stone, wood, iron, steel, and tin, all to build a better world. But alas, man has thwarted God's plans, and now, when God looks over the world, I think He must find the beautiful stone He gave us for a better world a mere monument over a tomb. And wood, he finds, is a million little crosses over Flanders Fields.[13] While iron, steel, and tin seem to race through the air to pierce the hearts of men. O, my soul doth cry aloud as the hand of Justice settles down on the human race. O God, have mercy, and look for the moments in human souls, for there the stone You gave us is the symbol of Thyself—Thou art the cornerstone of truth. And wood is the accidental expression of our redemption because Thou didst will to die on the cross of wood. Look upon iron, steel, and tin as the symbols in our souls: they are desire, will, and sin—these we hope to fashion into something beautiful for Thee. O God, have mercy on the world and look only in the souls of love who understand the symbol of stone, wood, iron, steel, and tin.

PRIESTS

Jesus said, "O, My priestly sons, My yoke, the sweetness and marvel of Holy Scripture placed upon your shoulder, is it too great to bear? Sweetness at times is heavy to bear in a world of sin, but the cross of worldliness is heavier still—so heavy at times you would think it would slay the thought of Eternal Justice and pierce the counsel bar of inspired teachings, unless your will asks conscience to rebuff the florid streams of the sinful world about you. Try to remember, when you are sorely tempted, the meditation on My words: 'You, My sons, have not chosen Me, but I have chosen you!'"

Jesus said, "Sons, take your cross (the body) and the Holy Scriptures

13 During the First World War, the battlefields in the region of Western Belgium and Northern France were named Flanders Fields. The Flanders Fields American Cemetery is located in Belgium.

(the voice of wisdom), and lift your voice and rejoice, for you alone are at the foot of Calvary with Me. Rejoice in your transfiguration in Me. Rejoice that I relive My life in you. Time, as you understand time, is very short. Return today, even though your staff is bent from earth's weary walk in pleasure fields. Rejoice in love's repentant gifts; rejoice, for you will be with Me in Heaven *now* and forever."

The Scriptures read, "God is Love." We know God's love because He gives—He creates—He is life—He is both death and life. Happy and at peace are the souls who learn how to reciprocate for all Christ's gifts in His way of Love. When souls know the wisdom of love, then masters of great art they have become!

This is an uncertain world, for the devil has visibly raised his ugly host—the atom bomb. Christians are sure of this—tomorrow a Mass will be offered somewhere in the world; it is a promise as long as time exists. God's heart in our priest's hands is ready to burst for the love of us—let us praise Him—let us love Him—let us obey Him, and His way of love will overshadow the ugly host of evil.

Zealousness based on fear, because of lack of wisdom, brings Me sorrow from My priests. Zealousness should be based on love and trust in Me above all else.

BLESSED MOTHER AND THE ROSARY

Morning Star, Queen of the Holy Rosary, are you weary with us who give so little for thy holy cause? We hear the cries for charity in this earth's trials, but how much more is needed for the poor souls who cry to thee from Purgatory, "Mother, deliver us—give us light eternal."

It seemed I heard our Blessed Mother say, "I catch the holy beads of prayer like petals rare from the many folded hands in prayer. There I place them in my soul where they flutter as captured doves of love, and in return I give my Son's eternal joy to grant thy least desire."

On each rosary bead I said a self-made prayer, "I love Thee Jesus—I love Thee Jesus." Slowly, the beads fell through my fingers like sands in an hourglass, and my heart repeated as each bead fell, "I love Thee Jesus, I love Thee Jesus." Then, in wonderment I said aloud, "Beloved Jesus, dost Thou not tire of the same words over and over again?" Jesus calmly answered, "I have never changed the melody of the sea. Its roar, tumble, and ceaseless hum are the same to Me in storm and calm, nor do I tire of its song."

ANGELS

O Holy angels and fair sentinels, I beg of thee tonight to find each rosary not in use and pray them all for this: as every soul slides into death may it see the holy cross, the sign of Christ, our God.

One by one the falling rosary beads bring to life the living prayer. It is indeed a chain of thought, all on the majestic King.

SACRED HEART OF JESUS

With Jesus I am enthroned on earth only for the day, to play, to live, to love, and to praise and adore Him. In my heart there will be no tomorrow. No more yesterdays and no more excuses from my heart in defense of self, regardless of circumstances or trials. These shall not be permitted to play upon the stage of His Sacred Heart.

O Sacred Heart, unfold Thy Light, for in Thy Light we see the way, the peace, and joy to follow Thee.

JESUS—THE MASTER

In His love of perfect obedience and order, I am longing in Him to live, in Him to breathe, and in Him to find freedom to brush through the great distances of my own soul, into the depths, heights, and delights of His sacred Soul, there to find deepest impressions of His love, where all claims of earth's freedom become a crown of liberation, happiness, and union with and in Him.

The Master said to me, "While we are absent one from another, remember I am always with you in and through all natural creation. Whenever thou dost look upon My creations and think of Me, there I'll be and in the voices of inspiration I'll tell thee of My love for thee. Let not thy soul mourn when I'm absent for a day, for I must test thy faithfulness to Me through the penalty of loneliness from time to time."

THE WAY OF LOVE

Jesus, teach me how to pray. If You were me, what would You say when trials against charity for friends seem to be the cross for the day? Jesus answered, "The gift of wisdom is not prayer for self; rather, it is prayer for the good of other souls. This way of prayer is of great reward; it is self-denial against personal gain and self-esteem. It is the way to My greater way of love."

O night of my soul, when art thou going to end? Jesus answered, "In the quiet darkness of a soul in trial, there I often listen to its spiritual progress or defeat."

Jesus said, "When religion ceases to be a joyous game with God, then it ceases to be religion."

Jesus said, "It is better to accomplish little deeds for My glory than even [to] desire the great and lofty."

Jesus said, "Bless one another; forgive one another, for in My Kingdom you are one reflected tone on the harp of My Heart. I have created you for My delights."

Jesus said,

"Cora, Cora do you hear Me?
I'm the Master at your side.
I'm footsore and weary.
My loved ones are not near Me."

Jesus said, "When souls cease to be a blockade to My graces, then Heaven will rejoice and Justice will bless."

LOYALTY

I asked in prayer, "Jesus, what is the meaning of loyalty?" Jesus answered, "Loyalty is counsel lived by those who counsel. Loyalty is the better disposition of all petitions when one asks in prayer, "Thy will be done." Loyalty is a robe of royal purple worn by those souls who love Me through a penitential life governed by rule of self-discipline."

Jesus said, "Upon all loyal hearts, my lips have traced a kiss of love. Through souls, I have known joys and each excruciating pain, for I live in My castles where trust is a key and pain the door."

SAINT ALOYSIUS GONZAGA

Place the emphasis of your life in Heaven, not this world.

"What is majesty?" Saint Aloysius seemed to answer, "Majesty is without form. Majesty is unattainable. Majesty to the finite mind is truly a beautiful joy—it is like a silver steed galloping wildly through space just to toss its beautiful mane for the fun of its joy alone. Majesty is to be beautifully worshipped, for it is the dress of the Eternal Father in His joy alone. Majesty cannot be possessed by finite souls, for it is a joy of eternal life."

Priest should be ambassadors of peace. His priests are ambassadors of peace.

To offer excuse for thine own neglect is like digging sand with a sieve—uninteresting and without accomplishment.

Saint Aloysius recited this poem to me:

O immersion of pain
Thou art like darts of rain
Sprinkled from the Master's hand
For her soul is like parched land.

O immersion of pain
Thou dost offer her all gain
If she will surrender her fear
And trust in the Master most dear.

O immersion of pain
She asks, "Dost thou have a name?
Jesus, is it the lowly name 'Surrender'?
And in pain to believe Thou art always near?"

O immersion of pain
Teach her how to gain
The crown of all honors
To be worn by pain-loving donors.

CORA'S PRAYERS

When nightshades find me in their lingering pause, O hide me there, great God. For in night's purpling sheen and clouds of gold, I'm sure to find in prayer the sound of Thy footsteps coming near.

Footsteps aroused because souls love.
Footsteps aroused because God loves souls.
Footsteps aroused because God is the artist of great souls.

Whispering thoughts, dear Holy Spirit, come from You tonight. Whispering thoughts so sure and true. Keep me in the path of light; O whispering thoughts, stay with me until I reach the other shore.

Holy Spirit be my light
Have mercy on my night
Holy Spirit pour forth Thy Light
Until it overcomes my night

Teach me, O my beloved Jesus, how to give to Thee the drink You crave—it is the kiss of a human soul.

While I knelt to adore Thee, my Jesus, near Thy tabernacle home, I felt You pass by and caress me. You wore a crown of petals rare—they shimmered like huge rubies in the light of Thy holy gaze, and as the minutes passed away one by one, the petals fell, leaving only a crown of brittle thorns to move Thy Holy Face in pain. Please, O my Jesus, with Thy holy grace, permit me to pick each petal up again and place them there to stay.

Tonight I long to hear Thy wonderful voice, Jesus, but my sins— what shall I do with them? They are barriers between us, Jesus—They are as dark as any night. O my Jesus, let my tears win for me a total pardon, better for me to kneel in freedom's love before Thee when in vigil's hour keeping I kneel in waiting for Thee.

I am lonely tonight for Thee, Beloved. Life no longer holds contentment for me, for Thou hast shown me Thy Holy Face, and in Thy Face the world did melt away. No beauty or pleasure remains. Even the gold of sunsets and the blue of ocean depths still my heart with longing for Thee, for they are now but tiny reflections from the light within Thy Holy Face.

Oh, imagination, thou dost seem like an intruder in God's house of quiet prayer. Please remain and listen to His voice of wisdom and rekindle thyself in His love of denials.

Dear holy angels, if I live in that last dreadful day when you come to separate the wicked from the just, remember me as one who loved Christ's Holy Name and tried to keep in mind the grace to fear all sin, hoping to attain eternal love.

O eyes of Jesus, what do I see in Thy tender gaze? When I look at Thee, I feel like and resemble a tiny ant suffering whilst it gazes into the brilliant heat of our earthy sun as it speeds across the sky. And in the nothingness of an ant I cry aloud, "O powerful constant and inexpressible glory, Thy gaze is a crucifixion of joy, a crucifixion of death to the world and a crucifixion of death made sweet and desirable, for only in real death can we fully understand Thy caressing gaze."

Rugged was the path He trod, yet on His way He greeted friends with a friendly nod. O God, lead me in Thy path—let not a friend find me without Thy smile and nod for them.

O holy and divine Artist, we pray Thee to chisel into our souls the wounds of Thy love for us. Never leave us without the prick of the chisel's pain.

O fires of divine love, clothe us for the Master of Majesty.

CORA'S POETIC PRAYERS

Mother dear, I have a care—
My cross today seems hard to bear.
Lend me thy heart all pure and bright—
Therein I'll hide until I overcome the night.

Tears, O dear friend, dry those tears,
For tears often fall when one alone fears.
To fear, little soul, it is but a heart full of care,
Cares from the world soon fall away when we reach
For the Master's hand—for He cares.

Happiness is a mood, a road, or goal in life,
Happiness is taking Jesus for a friend.
Happiness is actual sacrifice, without strife,
Happiness finds no dusty mood for happiness knows a Friend.

UNTITLED PRAYERS BY CORA EVANS

Light of my soul—don't fade away
Darkness of my soul—please burn away

Darkness in sins—thou art a crucible voice,
A voice of lamentations, despair, and of vice.

Light of my soul—burn brightly for Him,
As we near Heaven's Light with a song for Him.

A small voice sang from a grayish light
And begged for Light unknown to human sight.

The heavens' shores broke upon me with these words:
"Humility, poor soul, is the shroud of the world.

Humility in love feeds the flame of each soul
Humility in the light of His Light is our Sacred Host."

Eternal judge come into my heart—
Take Thy throne never to depart.
Govern my way, my will, my love

Into the many ways of the silent dove.
Teach me to follow Him without leaving a trace
Of self-pride and self-will in this earth's race.
Let me follow Him in the avenues of time—
As He wings away without a trace.
Help me in the race, better for me to be all Thine
In all climes[14]—wooded hills and rocky shores.
Help me to knock upon all human doors
And when I enter let me whisper in words of time
About Thy love in Thy Humanity
Thy Humanity is the master of all devotions
It is timeless peace, it is eternal peace
And through its wisdom of love all evils cease.

O solitude of darkness cover me—
O darkness which is solitude in God
Let me search in quietness alone in Thee,
Better for me to love and serve Thee, O my God.

O interior sea of my soul—
In darkness which is light, I love thee.
Light, Thou art Jesus shining in the sea of my soul.

Let me follow Mary
Never let me tarry.
Without the love of Mary
Our cross we could not carry.

O holy cross—
In vision's silence Thou art like flaming wings.

14 A region considered with reference to its climate

O holy cross—
Let my will in flaming love to the cross daily cling.

O holy cross—
In death take my love and form it into flaming wings.

O holy cross—
In life let me cling to Thee
In death let me sing to Thee.

Don't let perseverance sleep
In thy soul it lies deep
Gently awaken it with prayer.

Purity is as delicate as candle flame.
Protect it against the foes of darkness.
It is as fragile as breath of life;
Don't cast it into darkness.

ABOUT PRAYER

One hour of penance—a few falling tears bring us close to Heaven. Pray, O My friends, for this great hour of love to fall thy way, for it is Jesus passing by.

"All for Jesus" is a will-full and beautiful expression of loving crucifixion.

When thoughts of prayer prompt thy knee to bend, O soul, be thankful and obey, for God is passing by.

To live for Jesus is to feel possessed by Him, and to know and feel His divine possession is the grace of perfect joy.

O boundless sea, surely thy rhythm is the symbol of angels' prayer, ceaseless, sighing, climbing, reaching, teaching us by the mighty waves that ceaseless prayer in God's own way is the order of the universe.

To be aware of God's nearness is constant actual prayer.

Interior peace in prayer often listens to the tones of Christ's Heart as a harp of love.

Pray regularly—pray unhurriedly—pray intensely. Pray while smiling—pray while crying—pray while praying.

Friends of earth often say, "Fool, fool—only fools take this path." Their call of "fool" brings the flutter of despair and questioning of God. Certain friends can take us from God. Lord, you chose my friends, and I know meekness and calm will be Thy choice.

FAVORED EXPRESSIONS

A soul in sin is like unto a moth in anguish before a screen of darkness, fighting for its entrance to the light within the screen. Its fragile wings beating upon the screen in a noiseless rhythm, it soon weakens and falls to be forgotten, even in its pain of broken wings, because it had not learned to say, "I'm sorry, Jesus."

Jesus loves. Yes, Jesus loves. Oh, Jesus, mercy from Thy love while amends in penance done. I'll rise to greet Thy love!

Sentimentalists have pictured Christ as effeminate. What a disgrace! Let our anguish in penance plead pardon for the thoughts of such artists.

Jesus is all-visible. He is beauty all around us. It is His hand that leads us into paths of good. It is His hand that sifts our deeds of sin and good into His hourglass, time. His hand, oh yes, His hand clasps ours and begs for our confidence, hope, and trust that He will direct our paths of destiny.

Love wanes—love loves—only God never wavers.

Passive law is the will of man to freely open all its will to God through love, better to allow God in Spirit to roam as He wills, through us, by us, and with us.

Christ is the servant of grace—let me watch with what gentleness He serves—let me learn from His calm grace how to live, how to sing, how to cry, and how to die, for He did all these things first for us.

Love is noticeable in the calm peace of a prayerful eye. Love is God—

Shadow of Christ, don't follow me; rather let me follow Thee.

We are blessed beyond compare. We, too, have a pulpit—is it not the Master's hand?

God, the Warrior, disguised Himself in human flesh, better to fight for us—take up the command.

LOVE

O happy thought, to think I love a King, a King of glory, a King divine. O greater joy, to know a King loves me and that King found me an orphan outside the city wall, and in His personal kindness He bid me come and eat with Him at the table of the King of Kings!

The Remarkable Story of Cora Evans

Saints are known by their stories. Their lives were given freely to the Lord in response to the circumstances at the time, and for the good of the whole Church. They did not ask for or expect to be in the situations in which they found themselves. These men and women radiated the holiness of God dwelling within them. It is the story of their lives, how they responded to grace, their impact on others, combined with God's proof by miracles in their name that led the pope to declare, "We know for certain this person is with God in Heaven."

Only God can make a saint. At this stage there is no certainty that Cora Evans will become a canonized saint. Today, she is a Servant of God,[15] and her cause for Beatification and Sainthood is under way in the Diocese of Monterey, California.

Cora Evans was born July 9, 1904, and she passed away March 30, 1957. Her first mystical experience, an apparition of the Blessed Mother, took place when she was three years old. It was an event she could not fully comprehend and would never forget. Many years would pass before she understood the vision and the message.

Cora was raised a Mormon and was married to Maclellan Evans in the well-known Mormon Temple in Salt Lake City, Utah. That event was the turning point in her life. She left the secret ceremony disillusioned and disappointed with Mormonism, especially the doctrine

---

15 "A Catholic whose cause of beatification and canonization has been initiated is called Servant of God." *Sanctorum Mater*, Congregation for the Causes of Saints, Title II, Article 4, February 22, 2007.

that placed man-made gods above the God of Abraham. "I was without a God and religion but had gained a very wonderful husband. As I looked at him and learned to love him more and more, I resolved to help find a God for him. After ten years of searching, we found the One True God in the Roman Catholic Church."

During the ten years that followed the marriage ceremony, Cora and Mack had three children. They suffered the loss of a child, Bobby, when he was ten months old. Cora investigated many religions, but believed it would be a waste of time to even inquire about Catholicism. Although she no longer considered herself a Mormon, she held on to pervasive anti-Catholic warnings she learned growing up in Utah.

On December 9, 1934, Cora was quite ill. The family lived in Ogden, Utah, at the time. Cora was in bed and the radio was on the other side of the room. No one was home and she was too sick to get out of bed to change the station when the Catholic Hour began broadcasting. Despite her aversion to Catholicism, Cora was forced to listen to Monsignor Duane Hunt[16] talk about the Blessed Mother and the teachings of the Catholic faith. His message conflicted with the negative stories Cora had been told about Catholics. As soon as she recovered, Cora went to nearby St. Joseph Catholic Church to inquire about the faith and have her questions answered. This was a courageous move for a former Mormon. A series of meetings followed, including debates in her home between the parish priest, Father Edward Vaughn, and several Mormon bishops. Cora quickly became aware of the truth of Christianity and the obvious false stories told about Catholics. She appreciated Father Vaughn's demeanor and the clarity of his responses to questions about Catholic doctrine. Cora was baptized March 30, 1935, and received her first Holy Communion the next day. Mack and their daughters, LaVonne and Dorothy, followed her lead a few months later.

Cora influenced many Mormons to visit St. Joseph's, inviting them to open house gatherings. Years later, Father Vaughn wrote a letter

---

16 Most Reverend Duane G. Hunt (1884–1960), consecrated Bishop of the Diocese of Salt Lake City, October 28, 1937. Bishop Hunt visited Cora in her home in Boulder Creek, California, shortly before she passed away in 1957.

confirming that through Cora's evangelization efforts there were hundreds of conversions of Mormons to the Catholic faith.

VOW DAY FOR A MYSTIC

In July 1938, she had a profound mystical experience. Cora wrote about this event in the autobiography of her mystical life, titled "Captain of the Ship." During this deep ecstasy Cora made the choice to serve God for the rest of her life. She described the state of her soul as being intimately united to God, and referred to this as her *vow day*: "It was necessary for me to live my chosen vocation with Him as my companion. By loaning Jesus my humanity for Him to govern as well as dwell within, would make my life a living prayer for He was life, living life within me, and my body now dead to me was His living cross, His cross to take to Calvary, Calvary, the door to eternal life."

THE MOVE TO SOUTHERN CALIFORNIA AND SPIRITUAL GUIDANCE

Due to religious and cultural prejudices, it was virtually impossible for Cora's husband, also a convert, to hold down a job. In 1941 the family moved to Southern California. In retrospect, I recognize this as God's plan. Cora began having mystical experiences with much greater frequency. In response to her search for spiritual guidance, on February 20, 1945, Father Frank Parrish, S.J.[17] was appointed her confessor and spiritual director by the Provincial[18] of the Society of Jesus (Jesuits). The meeting took place at Loyola High School in Los Angeles.

On December 24, 1946, Jesus revealed the mission entrusted to Cora. She learned that she was to promulgate the Mystical Humanity

---

17 Fr. Frank Parrish, S.J. (1911–2003) is best known in Catholic circles for his blessing of terminally ill Fr. John A. Houle, S.J. with the relic of Blessed Claude la Colombiere on February 23, 1990. This led to a miraculous cure—a first class miracle. Colombiere, who had been the spiritual director of Saint Margaret Mary, was declared a saint and canonized by Pope John Paul II, May 31, 1992.

18 Fr. Joseph J. King, S.J. (1900–1986) served as provincial from January 1943 to August 1948. The geographic area served in 1945 included California, Arizona, Nevada and Utah.

of Christ, a way of prayer that encourages people to live with a heightened awareness of the indwelling presence of Jesus in their daily lives. It is Eucharistic spirituality, and Jesus promised to foster the devotion.

Father Frank served as the spiritual guide of Cora's soul for the rest of her life. His written account of events is testimony to Cora's heroic virtues and her reputation of sanctity.

Cora is considered a hidden mystic, and although there were many friends, including priests and religious, she was not known publically. There are many examples of visionaries who where unknown at the time of their death, including Saints Margaret Mary (devotion to the Sacred Heart of Jesus), Catherine Laboure (Miraculous Medal), and Sister Faustina (Divine Mercy). Like these women, there was never any publicity about Cora's private revelation.

The life story of Cora Evans, wife and mother, is that of a remarkable woman who practiced Christian virtues and earned a reputation for holiness. She became a daily communicant and one of her favorite devotions was the Stations of the Cross. At times she would say the stations in reverse, mirroring the way the Blessed Mother saw them as she walked home from the crucifixion.

Cora's gifts of mysticism: suffering the wounds of Christ, known as the stigmata; the phenomena of bi-location associated with deep insight, a mystical gift not fully understood; the fragrance of roses associated with her presence, known as the odor of sanctity; visionary experiences, known as ecstasy; and profound writings far beyond her education level are not in and of themselves sufficient grounds for the declaration of sainthood. It is the story of her life with the proof of heroic virtues that places everything else in context.

The Vatican granted *nihil obstat*[19] for the cause for Beatification and Canonization of the Servant of God, Cora Evans. The Diocese of Monterey, California, is proceeding with the investigation of her life and writings.

---

19 Nihil obstat (Latin "Nothing stand in the way") is a term used for the approval for a given process to proceed. Granted by Angelo Cardinal Amato, S.D.B., Prefect, *Congregation for the Causes of Saints*, Rome, Italy. Letter March 29, 2012.

PRAYER FOR THE INTERCESSION
OF CORA EVANS

Cora prayed that she would be given the same gift as Saint Therese of Lisieux, the Little Flower, spending her heaven on earth doing good, and promised to pray for all who asked for her intercession after first visiting the Blessed Sacrament. The Archbishop of San Francisco granted the IMPRIMATUR[20] for the intercessory prayer, written by Father Frank Parrish, S.J.

Dear Jesus, You blessed Cora Evans with many supernatural mystical gifts as a means of drawing us to a deeper and more intimate union with your Sacred Heart through Your Divine Indwelling, Your Mystical Humanity. I ask You through her intercession to help me in my special request (name the favor) and my efforts to do Your will here on earth and be with You, Your Blessed Mother, Saint Joseph and the whole Court of Heaven forever.

Say three times: the Our Father, Hail Mary, Glory Be to the Father.

THE MYSTICAL HUMANITY OF CHRIST

Cora prayed, "Please give me the grace to remember the vision and understanding in Thy wisdom to better relate to friends Thy hidden mystery of love for them . . . help me, Jesus, to write them as You would like them written for Thy glory to be better known among men." The purpose of her life, the suffering she endured, and her writings inspire us to live with awareness of the presence of Jesus. When you practice this way of prayer, known as the Mystical Humanity of Christ, you take Jesus with you wherever you go.

---

20 Imprimatur (Latin "it may be printed") approval to publish given by diocesan bishop provides assurance that the published text conforms to Church teaching. Granted Most Reverend George Niederauer, Archbishop of San Francisco. Letter February 18, 2011.

COMPELLED TO WRITE

Cora Evans felt compelled by our Lord to write and at the same time felt wholly unqualified to take on such a task. Due to childhood illnesses, she never completed a full schedule of elementary school, and with less than two years of high school her education was rudimentary at best. Add to that, she was thirty years old before she had any exposure to the Catholic faith and she passed away at age fifty-two. It is what transpired during the years following her conversion that is truly remarkable.

A mystic and a visionary, Cora was called up into the deepest state of prayer known as ecstasy and rapture, but what our Lord preferred to have known as *Divine Slumber*. It is a pure gift from God and the source of all private revelation. Because the revelation is private there is no burden of belief on Catholics to accept it.

Cora's diary reveals that our Lord entrusted her with the responsibility to write. She suffered greatly for the privilege. After an experience of ecstasy, which might last for many hours, Cora would sit at the typewriter and attempt to capture the stories revealed to her.

The Refugee from Heaven is the greatest story ever known. Cora Evans recounts the life of Jesus Christ as an eyewitness, beginning with the first meeting between Jesus and Peter, on the shores of Mount Carmel Bay. With vivid detail and dialogue, this unique account breathes new life into well-known figures of the Gospels. Readers gain startling insights into Mary of Magdala's conversion, Herod's ferocious personality, and John the Baptist's courage. Experience the awe of the disciples in the Upper Room at the Last Supper, and stand in the holy sepulcher at the moment of the Resurrection. With a book that is sure to renew appreciation for the loving Heart of Jesus, the author has created an enduring masterpiece.

For more information about the cause for Cora Evans, the availability of her writings, or speaking engagements and parish retreats contact *Michael McDevitt, Custodian for the Writings of Cora Evans, Mike@ CoraEvans.com* and visit *CoraEvans.com* AND *ParishRetreat.org.*